EVALUATING VIEWPOINTS:
CRITICAL THINKING IN
UNITED STATES HISTORY SERIES

TEACHER'S GUIDE

BOOK FOUR
SPANISH-AMERICAN WAR
TO
VIETNAM WAR

KEVIN O'REILLY

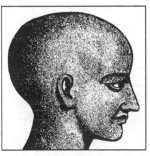

© 1985, 1991
CRITICAL THINKING BOOKS & SOFTWARE
(formerly Midwest Publications)
P.O. Box 448 • Pacific Grove • CA 93950-0448
Phone 800-458-4849 • FAX 408-393-3277
ISBN 0-89455-420-4
Printed in the United States of America
Reproduction rights granted for single-classroom use only.

TABLE OF CONTENTS

ABOUT THE AUTHOR

Kevin O'Reilly is a social studies teacher at Hamilton-Wenham Regional High School in Massachusetts. He was named by *Time* magazine and the National Council for the Social Studies as the 1986 Outstanding Social Studies Teacher in the United States. In addition to these four volumes on Critical Thinking in United States History, Mr. O'Reilly is the coauthor of *Critical Viewing: Stimulant to Critical Thinking* (also published by Midwest Publications/Critical Thinking Press & Software) and the author of "Escalation," the computer simulation on the Vietnam War (Kevin O'Reilly, 6 Mason Street, Beverly, MA 01915). Mr. O'Reilly, who has a Master of Arts Degree in History, is an editor of the *New England Journal of History*. He conducts workshops throughout the United States on critical thinking, critical viewing, and decision making.

> **FOR**
> Mom and Dad and
> Helen and Charlie

ACKNOWLEDGMENTS

I would like to thank the following for their help: the Hart Nautical Museum at the Massachusetts Institute of Technology for allowing me to make a photocopy of a diagram of the *Lusitania* (Lesson 8); Ron Lovett for his ideas and suggestions on World War I (Lesson 9); Peter Temin, economics professor at the Massachusetts Institute of Technology, for reviewing the interpretations on the causes of the Great Depression (Lesson 14) and explaining some of the more difficult economic problems; Martin Herz for writing a lengthy review of my original lesson on the origins of the Cold War (Lesson 21); Nicole Fasciano, Cathy Luxton, and Garrett Sawyer for their research papers on the Kennedy assassination which helped me write the two interpretations (Lesson 29); and Robert Swartz, professor in the Critical and Creative Thinking Program at the University of Massachusetts at Boston for his suggestions on reasoning, especially cause and effect, and generalizations.

INTRODUCTION

Overview of This Section

This teacher's guide contains an introduction; reproducible introductory lessons for each skill covered in the series; suggested teaching strategies and answers for each lesson in the student text; and test questions. The introduction includes:

1. an introduction to the process of critical thinking;

2. a rationale for the series;

3. a description of the role of the teacher, including an overview of the *Teacher's Guide*, suggestions for classroom methods for teaching critical thinking in history, and various suggestions for evaluating student progress;

4. a description of the role of the student, including an overview of the student text;

5. a chart of the scope and sequences of skills developed in this text;

6. a bibliography of sources on critical thinking.

What Is Critical Thinking?

One author calls critical thinking "reasoned judgment." For the purposes of this series, critical thinking is *judging* the worth of claims or arguments. It involves judgment, assessment, and evaluation. The critical thinker has a healthy skepticism and asks probing questions; the non-critical thinker is likely to jump to conclusions and believe whatever is claimed.

Critical thinking is not the same as creative thinking, brainstorming, problem solving, decision making, conceptualizing, or Bloom's taxonomy—although it is involved in the judgment phase of problem solving and decision making. Neither is it the same as asking students to compare and contrast or to categorize—for those activities do not require students to evaluate the comparisons made or categories delineated.

Only level six (evaluation) of Bloom's taxonomy involves critical thinking. Level four (analysis) is so important to evaluation of arguments, however, that some of these skills are also directly taught in these books.

The following analysis and evaluation skills are included in the series.

> — **Analysis Skills** —
>
> • Differentiating between conclusions and reasons
>
> • Identifying types of reasoning
>
> • Identifying sources of information
>
> • Classifying parts of an argument based on cue words, value words, emotional words, and change-of-direction words
>
> • Identifying assumptions and value judgments
>
> — **Evaluation Skills** —
>
> • Evaluating the relevance of reasons to conclusions
>
> • Evaluating types of reasoning
>
> • Evaluating sources
>
> • Evaluating assumptions and value judgments

Overall, then, the critical thinker asks, "Why should I believe this?" and offers reasoned judgments in answer to that question. These books are meant to arm students with the critical-thinking skills necessary to make reasoned judgments, to prod them into asking questions, and to give them the confidence both to ask questions and to offer judgments.

About This Series

This four-volume series, Evaluating Viewpoints: Critical Thinking in United States History, is intended to improve critical thinking through evaluation of conflicting viewpoints of United States history. The books are chronological, each covering a particular time period.

Book 1: Colonies Through Constitution
   (1492–1789)

Book 2: New Republic Through Civil War
   (1790–1865)

Book 3: Reconstruction Through Progressivism
   (1865–1914)

Book 4: Spanish-American War Through Vietnam War
   (1900–1980)

There is not, however, chronological coverage within each book. Each lesson is a self-contained problem that can be "plugged in" at any point in a corresponding history unit.

These books are thus meant to supplement other curriculum materials, not to be the sole text for a course.

As mentioned in the introduction of the student text, the root word of history is *story*. In this series, emphasis is on helping students see that the "story" of history can be told in different ways and that values, attitudes, perceptions, and selection all shape the way people see the past. These books are intended to show students that historical subject matter is not some unchanging, agreed upon, and complete subject to be memorized, but rather is changing, selective, fragmentary, and open to interpretation.

The target of this series is understanding, not memorizing. Studies in cognitive psychology indicate that memorization lasts only a short time. Focusing on problems, thinking, and understanding helps students remember the content of history much longer.

The Role of the Teacher
About the Teacher's Guide

The *Teacher's Guide* contains:

1. an introduction to the series;
2. reproducible worksheets for introducing each skill;
3. objectives, teaching ideas, and suggested answers for each lesson;
4. possible test questions and suggested answers.

Twelve skill worksheets are included in the *Teacher's Guide* of each book in the series. These can be used to promote a questioning attitude (Worksheet A), introduce particular skills (Worksheets B–J), or serve as general worksheets for evaluating any film or written argument (Worksheets K–L). The teaching ideas and the suggested answers are intended as guidance for the teacher, not as rigid lesson plans or right answers. The emphasis is on thinking, not on "correct" answers.

A key element in the emphasis on teaching, practicing, and repeating critical thinking skills is the "Scope and Sequence of Skills" chart on pages 12–13. Once you have decided which skills to teach, this chart will serve as a quick reference to their location in each book and to help you select appropriate lessons for practice and repetition. Values are included under "Assumptions" in the scope-and-sequence chart, since they are a kind of assumption about the way the world should be. Those lessons focusing on values are marked with a "v."

Some skills are not represented on the scope-and-sequence chart. Although these skills are not **explicitly** taught in any lesson in the book, they are a part of many of the problem lessons. For example, finding the main idea is an important part of evaluating the interpretations in the book. The importance of using key words for encoding parts of arguments is also a part of many problem lessons, but is never explicitly taught in any specific lesson. For further information on critical thinking, refer to the Bibliography of Sources on Critical Thinking on page 11 in this book.

Classroom Methods for Teaching Critical Thinking in History

Unlike other anthologies of opposing viewpoints, this series focuses on how to analyze and evaluate arguments. In improving athletic performance, coaches know that a systematic approach works best. Skills must be broken down and their components explained; the athlete has to try the skill with the guidance of the coach; the athlete must repeatedly practice the skill; and, finally, the skills must be applied in the athletic contest. This same method is used in these books to teach skills of critical thinking. Each skill is broken down and explained in the "Guide to Critical Thinking"; with the guidance of the teacher and/or other students, the student tries the skill on worksheets; additional worksheets provide practice as the student repeats the skill; and, finally, the student applies the skill to new opposing-viewpoint problems. This pattern of skill instruction is outlined below.

Pattern of Skill Instruction

1. INITIAL PROBLEM

In the books in this series, students are confronted with a historical problem from the student text. Since the problem consists of opposing viewpoints, students are forced to evaluate the viewpoints to arrive at a conclusion. This raises the need to learn to think critically in deciding which viewpoint to believe.

2. FAMILIAR EXAMPLE

The teacher gives the class an everyday problem, either from the "Guide to Critical Thinking" or an introductory worksheet, on the skill involved in step 1. Familiar examples make it easier for students to learn the skill.

3. METACOGNITION

This step offers direct teaching of analysis and/or evaluation skills. As the class discusses answers to the familiar problem in step 2, they discuss how class members arrived at their answers. The focus here is on *metacognition*—thinking about thinking, not about the content of the problem—and the components are taught directly. What is involved in performing the skill? What are the steps in the skill? What are the criteria for evaluation? A diagram of the steps or criteria is then posted in the classroom and/or drawn in the "skills" section of students' notebooks. Ideally, the students, guided by the teacher, will identify the components of the skill; those the class cannot identify can be taught directly by the teacher using the "Guide to Critical Thinking."

4. GUIDED PRACTICE

The students are referred back to the historical problem in step 1 and directed to discuss its evaluation in light of the skill they have learned. The students employ the skill on the problem and on worksheets with the guidance of the teacher and other students.

5. MASTERY

Students repeatedly practice the skill on additional worksheets and in class discussions.

6. EXTENSION

As the course progresses, students extend the skill as they apply it to new historical problems.

Class Discussions

From this emphasis on specific critical thinking skills, it can be seen that class discussions of the opposing viewpoints presented in the books are not to be free-for-alls, where all opinions are equally good. Students are expected to employ the skills learned in previous classes, to question assertions made by their classmates, and to defend their own assertions with evidence and reasons. This is a far cry from an emphasis on right answers. In this series, the emphasis is on good thinking, not on right answers.

Adaptation

Obviously, some of the lessons in this text are more difficult than others. Teachers can make easy lessons more challenging by eliminating step-by-step questions or worksheets or by making students produce their own examples to illustrate particular skills. Lessons that are too difficult for some classes can be made easier by doing only a portion of the lesson, by focusing on only a single skill, or by giving students the step-by-step worksheet on the topic. Refer to teaching suggestions on specific lessons for further guidance in the difficulty level of each lesson within this book.

Using the "Guide to Critical Thinking"

The "Guide to Critical Thinking," the first unit in each student text, is meant to help teachers with the direct instruction of key elements of the various critical thinking skills. These key skills are summarized in the chart on pages 12–13.

Although the Guide touches on numerous skills related to the evaluation of interpretations or arguments, it focuses on four of these skills: evaluation of evidence, evaluation of cause-and-effect reasoning, evaluation of comparison reasoning (analogy), and evaluation of generalizations. A grasp of these four argument components is an enormous help in the students' ability to think critically.

The section on *evidence* emphasizes the idea of sources of information. Rather than distinguishing between evidence, which has a source, and information, which provides no source, students are simply instructed to ask, "Is there a source?" whenever they encounter information in support of a claim. If not, they are to note that weakness. If yes, they are to evaluate it. Introductory Worksheet B (pp. 33–34 in this book) provides a concrete problem for determining and evaluating evidence.

In the section on *reasoning*, it is again important to note that students are not only taught to identify the type of reasoning but also to evaluate it. It is not enough that a student says, "This is a cause-and-effect argument." The student must also say whether it is a strong or weak cause-and-effect argument and give reasons for saying so. A concrete problem for introducing cause-and-effect reasoning can be found in the teaching ideas for Introductory Worksheet E (pp. 39–40 in this book).

The section on *evaluating comparisons* (analogies) is not the same as the activity of compare and contrast. This critical thinking skill focuses on evaluating comparison arguments, or what is sometimes called analogic reasoning. For example, asking students to compare and contrast the fighting in Nicaragua in the 1980s with the Vietnam War is very different from asking them to evaluate the argument "The United States should not be involved in fighting in Nicaragua because it will turn into another Vietnam." Although both assignments involve basic knowledge of the two situations, the second assignment requires students to identify the type of reasoning used and to implement comparison and contrast without being cued to do so (as in the first assignment). A concrete problem for introducing comparison reasoning is in the teaching ideas for Introductory Worksheet F (pp. 41–42 in this book).

The term *generalization*, rather than *sample reasoning*, is used for this skill. Use the pizza example on page 8 of the student book as a concrete problem for introducing generalizations. Ask "Suppose you bit into a pizza and the bite was cold. What might you conclude about the pizza?" The strength of a generalization can be determined by asking, "How large and representative is the sample?" Some people, however, believe that randomness is better than representativeness as a method for achieving an accurate sample. In any event, you might want to mention to your students that randomness is also a commonly accepted method of sampling.

Fallacies, although included with each type of reasoning, are not emphasized either in the Guide or in the lessons. Simply teaching students a few questions to ask (and the willingness to ask them) within several broad areas of reasoning will usually be more helpful than teaching them a larger number of fallacies and having them try to fit real arguments into one of these fallacies.

Several points emphasized in the ARMEAR model on page 18 in the student text are not emphasized elsewhere in the Guide. One such point is questions about the author (A); the second is relevant information (R). Students should be taught to bring any information that might be relevant to bear on the topic. They may, of course, have difficulty determining what is relevant. Additionally, they are not in the habit of seeing the relevance of one topic to another. To encourage the habit of thinking about what might be relevant to a historical problem, a number of lessons include relevant information sheets. Students who don't use the sheets can't do a complete analysis of the arguments. Encouraging this habit of calling on what they know helps students view history as a fund of knowledge to be drawn upon to help provide perspective on other, similar issues. History thereby becomes more meaningful.

Skill Transfer

Many of the worksheets contain both everyday and historic argument examples. This mixture is intended to promote transfer of the skills learned into other areas of the students' lives. Teachers can facilitate this transfer of critical thinking skills learned in history class to other subject areas by having students debate topics then analyze the reasoning they used in the debate. When students realize that they use the same reasoning elements in their own thinking, they are more likely to transfer them into other areas of their lives. Another important method for promoting skill transfer is to listen carefully to student chatter before class starts. If you can ask a question on the use of a particular type of reasoning on a topic heard in a student conversation, you will connect the skill learned in history to the students' everyday lives.

Evaluation

Test questions are provided at the end of this teacher's guide, and the many problem sheets in the student text provide even more possible test questions. Of course, teachers should consider the viewpoints in the longer problems for essay assignments. These can be evaluation essays, such as "Evaluate Historian A's argument on immigration. In your essay identify and evaluate two pieces of evidence and two types of reasoning."

Writing and Thinking

Writing skills are an important part of this curriculum, and students should be held accountable for their critical thinking skills when they write any essay assignment. A sample student assignment might be, "Write a minimum 250-word essay on the main cause of the American Revolution. In your essay you are to show what makes a strong cause, support your case with one piece of evidence, and explain why this is strong evidence." Students must learn how to construct strong arguments in addition to evaluating the arguments made by others.

Overview of Book 4

Book 4 is comprised of the "Guide to Critical Thinking" (Unit 1), ten introductory worksheets, and twenty-nine lessons divided into four units. Lessons 1–9 are in the United States as a World Power unit; Lessons 10–16 in the 1920s and the New Deal unit; Lessons 17–22 in the Foreign Policy Since 1945 unit; and Lessons 23–29 in the Modern American Society and Politics unit. The table of contents and the scope-and-sequence chart show the specific topic and the emphasized skills of each lesson.

> Lessons with titles phrased as questions are historical problems rather than worksheets. These problems involve numerous skills and focus on historical issues; worksheets focus on a single skill and mix familiar with historical content, rather than considering overriding historical questions.

The first four skills (evidence, cause-and-effect, comparison, and generalization) involve both identification and evaluation. A few lessons focus on either identification or evaluation, but most consider both.

Some teachers will prefer to use just the historical problem lessons. As mentioned above, these are the last three or four lessons in each unit (Lessons 6–10, 13–16, 20–22, and 27–29). These problem lessons can be used to teach a variety of skills and are interesting topics to study. Worksheet lessons, on the other hand, provide practice in particular skills to help students do more complete analyses of the interpretations in the problem lessons. The worksheet lessons provide sequencing of each skill.

The list of major sources used (p. 167 in the student text) shows that the viewpoints in Book 4 are based on major interpretations: Colin Simpson and Thomas Bailey on the *Lusitania*; the Nye Committee and Charles Seymour on the United States entry into World War I; Milton Friedman and Peter Temin on the causes of the Great Depression; Paul Conkin and William Leuchtenburg on the New Deal; Gar Alperovitz and Herbert Feis on the atomic bomb; John Lewis Gaddis, Martin Herz, and Gabriel Kolko on the origins of the cold war; Frances Fitzgerald, David Halberstam, Guenter Lewy and William Westmoreland on the Vietnam War; Richard Rovere and Robert Steele on Senator Joe McCarthy; and Mark Lane, David Lifton and the Warren Commission report on the Kennedy assassination.

While these are all well known interpretations, some are highly controversial. People may argue that some of the interpretations are quite fanciful, not credible enough to even bring to student attention. But if some of the interpretations are weak, let the students recognize their weaknesses. Good arguments are judged good because they are stronger than bad arguments. Students need to encounter and evaluate both.

The Role of the Student

The student book contains the "Guide to Critical Thinking" and twenty-nine lessons involving critical thinking. The "Guide to Critical Thinking" is intended to be used when students have a need to learn the components of a particular skill. While some may find it worthwhile to read through the whole Guide to get an overview of the skills involved in argument evaluation, it is not recommended that students study all the various skills at once. Rather, they should refer to the part of the Guide that explains the skill they are currently learning.

The historical lessons consist of both a short problem section for practicing skills (1–2 pages each) and longer historical problems (2–25 pages each) with opposing viewpoints. Paragraphs in longer viewpoints are numbered to make discussion and referencing easier.

Particular skills, especially generalizations and cause-and-effect reasoning, are explained with visual models. These have proven helpful for some, and students regularly use them to help evaluate arguments on tests.

These books focus on formulating good arguments as well as evaluating arguments offered by others. In this way, students should begin to question their own assumptions, points of view, and prejudices. This self-criticism, referred to by Richard Paul as "critical thinking in the strong sense," is an important, if difficult, goal to achieve.

Students should begin to see historical knowledge as changing, selective, fragmentary, and open to question. This change in student attitudes about the nature of historical knowledge (epistemology) is as important as their mastery of critical thinking skills. Beginning with Worksheet A, students should be encouraged, even expected, to question viewpoints presented. The problem format helps students see history the way it really is and to ask questions. It also makes history much more interesting.

Bibliography of Sources on Critical Thinking

Beyer, Barry. *Practical Strategies for the Teaching of Thinking.* Boston: Allyn and Bacon, 1987.

——— "Teaching Critical Thinking: A Direct Approach." *Social Education* 49 (April 1985): 297–303.

Bloch, Marc. *The Historian's Craft.* New York: Random House, 1953.

Bloom, Benjamin S., ed. *Taxonomy of Educational Objectives, Handbook I: Cognitive Domain.* New York: David McKay, 1956.

Carr, Edward Harlett. *What Is History?* New York: Random House, 1961.

Copi, Irving. *Introduction to Logic.* 5th ed. New York: Macmillan, 1978.

Costa, Arthur. "Teaching For, Of, and About Thinking." In *Developing Minds: A Resource Book for Teaching Thinking.* Edited by Arthur L. Costa, 20–24. Alexandria, VA: Association for Supervision and Curriculum Development, 1985.

——— and Lawrence Lowery. *Techniques for Teaching Thinking.* Pacific Grove, CA: Midwest, 1989.

Crossley, David J., and Peter Wilson. *How to Argue.* New York: Random House, 1979.

Fisher, David Hackett. *Historians' Fallacies: Toward a Logic of Historical Thought.* New York: Harper and Row, 1970.

Gustavson, Carl. *A Preface to History.* New York: McGraw-Hill, 1955.

Norris, Stephen. "The Reliability of Observation Statements." *Rational Thinking Reports*, No. 4. Urbana, IL: University of Illinois, 1979.

——— and Robert Ennis. *Evaluating Critical Thinking.* Pacific Grove, CA: Midwest, 1989.

O'Reilly, Kevin. "Teaching Critical Thinking in High School U.S. History." *Social Education* 49 (April 1985): 281–4.

——— "Vietnam: A Case Study for Critical Thinking" (videotape). Pleasantville, NY: Educational Audiovisual, 1989.

Paul, Richard. "Critical Thinking: Fundamental to Education for a Free Society." *Educational Leadership* 42 (September 1984): 4–14.

Roden, Philip. *The Elusive Truth.* Glenview, IL: Scott-Foresman, 1973.

Sanders, Norris. *Classroom Questions: What Kinds?* New York: Harper and Row, 1966.

Swartz, Robert and D. N. Perkins. *Teaching Thinking: Issues and Approaches.* Pacific Grove, CA: Midwest, 1989.

Weddle, Perry. *Argument: A Guide to Critical Thinking.* New York: McGraw-Hill, 1977.

Scope and Sequence of Skills • Book 4

Abbreviations used in this chart are as follows: (**TG**)–Teacher's Guide; (**GTC**)–"Guide to Critical Thinking," Unit 1 in Student Book; (**v**)–Values; (**f**)–Fallacy.

Lesson	Topic	Evidence	Cause/Effect	Comparison	Generalization	Assumption	Relevant Information	Proof and Debating
Concrete Example		TG 14	TG 19	TG 39	GCT 8	—	—	—
Explanation		GCT 2	GCT 5	GCT 7	GCT 8	GCT 15	GCT 18	GCT 11
Introductory Worksheets								
A	Bermuda Triangle	▦	▦		▦	▦		
B, C, D	Evaluating Evidence	▦	▦					
E	Cause and Effect Reasoning		▦					
F, G	Evaluating Comparisons			▦				
H	Evaluating Generalizations				▦			
I, J	Identifying Assumptions					▦		
United States as a World Power								
1	Foreign Policy	▦						
2	Foreign Policy	▦						
3	Foreign Policy		▦					
4	Spanish-American War	▦		▦				
5	Foreign Policy				▦			
6	Spanish-American War	▦		▦	▦	▦		
7	Imperialism	▦		▦	▦			▦
8	Lusitania					▦ (v)		
9	World War I	▦ (f)	▦			▦		▦ (f)

Scope and Sequence of Skills • Book 4 (continued)

1920s and the New Deal

Lesson	Topic	Evidence	Cause/Effect	Comparison	Generalization	Assumption	Relevant Information	Proof and Debating
10	1920s and 1930s	■						
11	1920s and 1930s			■				
12	Prohibition and 1920s		■					
13	Sacco and Vanzetti	■						
14	Causes of Depression	■	■			■	■	
15	New Deal		■			■		
16	New Deal		■		■	■		

Foreign Policy Since 1945

Lesson	Topic	Evidence	Cause/Effect	Comparison	Generalization	Assumption	Relevant Information	Proof and Debating
17	Cold War	■						
18	Cold War				■	■ (v)		
19	Foreign Policy Since 1945		■	■	■			■ (f)
20	Atom Bomb	■	■	■	■	■ (v)	■	■
21	Origins of the Cold War	■	■	■	■ (f)	■ (v)		■ (f)
22	Vietnam			■	■	■ (v)		

Modern American Society and Politics

Lesson	Topic	Evidence	Cause/Effect	Comparison	Generalization	Assumption	Relevant Information	Proof and Debating
23	McCarthyism	■						
24	Urban Riots		■					
25	Society and Politics		■	■	■			■
26	Civil Rights		■		■			
27	Black Mobility		■				■	
28	Working Women		■				■	
29	Kennedy Assassination	■	■					

UNIT 1
INTRODUCTORY LESSONS FOR SKILL DEVELOPMENT

Worksheet A: The Bermuda Triangle

Objectives

To increase skepticism of what is read, seen, or heard
To develop inclination and ability to question statements

Teaching Ideas
  PREPARATION

Give students copies of the first page of the worksheet (page 31) and ask them to write their reaction to it. Do not allow discussion at this point. Check to make sure everyone has written something. If some students say they don't understand what to write, tell them to write down how they feel about the reading, but don't go into any more detail. The whole idea is to avoid letting them know what reactions you are looking for.

  USING THE WORKSHEET

Some students will accept the argument in the handout without any criticisms. Many students feel that anything written down must be true. When the discussion begins they will see that some of their classmates were more skeptical and that the argument should not have been blindly accepted.

When you distribute copies of the Relevant Information sheet (page 32), this lesson in skepticism should be reinforced. After students read the relevant information, the author's argument should look very weak.

  EXTENDING THE LESSON

This reading might also be used to teach a number of other skills, such as finding the main idea, identifying value and emotional words, identifying assumptions and fallacies, and evaluating evidence.

Suggested Analysis

The author argues that one hundred ships go down each year, but does not compare that to the number of ships in the area (ten thousand distress calls) or to the number of sinkings in other areas of the ocean.

In paragraph 6 the author uses the "leading question technique" when he asks why pilot Cosner did not go on Flight 19. Maybe Cosner was constipated or had the flu. The later suggestion that he had a "peculiar feeling" is not really argued or supported by evidence. Similarly, the author suggests that the Navy is covering up the situation by not saying anything about it. But maybe the Navy has not bothered to deny it because the whole theory is so ridiculous.

Worksheet B: Evaluating Evidence

Objectives

To increase ability in identifying evidence
To increase ability in evaluating evidence

Teaching Ideas
INTRODUCING THE SKILL

To introduce the skills of identifying and evaluating evidence, take five students into the hallway, out of the class's sight, and tell them they are going to role play a murder. Have three students stay near your classroom door, one student go 25 feet down the hall in one direction, and the other student go 25 feet in the opposite direction. Tell them they are to watch carefully. Hand one of the three students by the door a pen and tell him or her to point it at one of the other students in the hall and yell, "Bang!" Tell the "murdered" student to fall down.

Bring the five students back together, and tell them the rest of the class is going to ask them questions to figure out who committed the crime. Only the murderer may lie; the witnesses (everyone else in the hall) must tell the truth. Tell the other witnesses they must tell everything they know. They are not to hide information or try to confuse the class.

When using this in class, substitute the corresponding student name for each of the roles in italics.

Re-enter the classroom with the five students. Tell the class that *the victim* was just killed, and have that person sit down. Tell the class that their task is to figure out who did it by questioning the four witnesses. [At some point a student may ask where the murder weapon is. If so, produce the pen (tell them it's a poison-dart gun) and ask if they have any questions about the weapon. If they ask about fingerprints, say that only *the murderer's* fingerprints are on it.] Later, tell the class that you have a letter, dated a month ago, written by *the murderer* to a close friend saying he or she was going to get even with *the victim*. Don't be discouraged if the students don't ask very good questions. Even advanced classes have had difficulty with this introductory exercise.

After ten to fifteen minutes, tell the class that you're going to stop talking about who committed the murder and, instead, talk about the skill involved in trying to decide who did it. This is the metacognitive stage. Ask the class what they think evidence is. [Based on this activity: statements by witnesses, objects that were part of the event, or written documents.]

The best way to get at the criteria for evaluating evidence is to ask the general question: How did you decide which evidence to believe? This way the class will generate the criteria themselves. If the general question proves too difficult you can ask more specific questions:

Ask the class why they didn't believe *the murderer* when s/he said s/he didn't do it. [S/he had a reason to lie to protect him- or herself.] Suppose *the murderer* said *a witness* did it, and *that witness* said *the murderer* did it, and that's all the class knew. Could they have told who was guilty? [No.] So why did they believe *that witness* over *the murderer*? [Because other witnesses supported *that witness's* version by saying *the murderer* did it.] Suppose a third witness was around the corner when the murder occurred. Would that strengthen or weaken his/ her evidence? [Weaken it.] Why? [The testimony is now given by someone who did not see the crime—a secondary source.] Is *the murderer* more likely to tell the truth in the trial or in a letter to a friend? [This is tricky, but the private letter is generally more reliable.]

REVIEWING THE SKILL

Write the criteria for evaluating evidence (see section on **Evaluation** in the "Guide to Critical Thinking," student text, page 3) on the board and have students copy it into their notebooks. You could also ask a volunteer to make a poster to remind students of the criteria (below).

EVALUATING EVIDENCE

Is there a source for the information?

If no, the information is unsupported and weakened.

If yes, evaluate it:

     P — primary or secondary?

     R — reason to lie or exaggerate?

     O — other evidence to verify this evidence?

     P — public or private?

This process of making posters for the classroom can be repeated for other skills and their criteria.

USING THE WORKSHEET

When the class has completed the role-play activity and the discussion, you can pass out Worksheet B (pp. 33–34) as an immediate follow-up on evaluating evidence. Tell the students they are going to practice what they have just learned about evaluating evidence.

Suggested Answers

• The jury was probably right in its guilty verdict.

Point out that making the historical judgment that Lucky stabbed John Jones is not the same as finding him guilty in court. In history, unlike in court, we do not have to prove something "beyond a reasonable doubt," but rather provide enough evidence to show that the person probably did it. In other words, we might say we think Lucky committed the murder, but should have been found "not guilty" in court. We do not presume innocence in history as we do in trials.

A. Statements are numbers 1–10, 12, and 15– 17.

B. Documents are numbers 14 and 18.

C. Objects are numbers 11 and 13.

• The evidence is evaluated as follows.

> **P**—Is the evidence primary?
>
> **R**—Does the person have a reason to lie?
>
> **O**—Is there other supporting evidence?
>
> **P**—Is the evidence private?

	4	7	10	11	14	17	18
P	no	yes	yes	yes	yes	no	no
R	yes	yes	no	no	no	no	no
O	no	yes	yes	yes	yes	yes	yes
P	no	no	no	yes	yes	yes	yes

• Since evidence 18 is private and seems to have no reason to lie, it is more reliable than evidence 4. Not foolproof; just more likely to be reliable.

Worksheet C: Sources and Evidence

Objectives

To identify sources
To evaluate evidence

Teaching Ideas
USING THE WORKSHEET

Students must first determine if a source for the information is given. Then, if there is a source, they are to evaluate it according to the four questions explained in the Worksheet C handout.

Distribute copies of the worksheet and ask the students to complete as much as they can. Remind them that a longer explanation of evidence can be found on pages 2–4 in Unit 1 of their book.

When students have filled in as much of the sheet as they can, have them compare answers in groups of three. Finally, discuss the worksheet as a class.

Suggested Answers

1. Since the statement gives no source for the information, it cannot be further evaluated. Thus, the evidence is not well supported.

   [You will need to point out to some students that even though a specific figure ($15 million) is used, we do not know where the figure came from; no source is given.]

2. The scorebook is the source for the statistic. **P**—it is a primary source, since the scorekeeper had to be at the games; **R**—there is no reason for the scorebook (or scorekeeper) to lie about hits and times at bat (batting average); **O**—there is no other evidence given to support the claim that Kurt is a great hitter; **P**—it is a public statement. **Overall**, this would be considered a reliable source.

3. The three workers' statements at the public hearings are the source. **P**—the workers say they saw payoffs, so they are primary sources; **R**—the workers might have motives to lie or exaggerate if they do not like Mayor Pratt; **O**—the three workers verify each other; **P**—these are public statements. **Overall**, the fact that three people were willing to risk testifying about the corruption does carry some weight, although the evidence is not as reliable as that in problem 2.

4. There is no source given for the information, so it is not well supported.

Worksheet D: Evaluating Evidence — PROP

Objectives

To evaluate sources of evidence

Teaching Ideas
USING THE WORKSHEET

Pass out the worksheet. Ask the students to fill it in then discuss their answers as a class. If students are confused about any of the criteria, the following questions may help them clarify their evaluations.

QUESTIONS FOR DETERMINING EVIDENCE

- To determine if someone is a **primary source**, ask, "Was this person at the location when the event occurred, or was she talking about herself?"

- To determine if someone has a **reason to lie**, ask, "Did this person make him- or herself look good by the statement?" [Why would s/he lie to make him or herself look bad?]

- To determine if there is **other supporting evidence**, ask, "Who said this? Did any other people say the same thing?"

- To determine if the evidence is **public**, ask, "Did this person make the statement to influence anyone else? Does he or she think anyone other than the person spoken to would hear what was said?"

Suggested Answers

1. Yu-chi **P**—is a primary source; **R**—has a reason to lie; **O**—presents no supporting evidence; **P**—the statement is public, meant to influence his father. **Overall**, the evidence is not very reliable because of the reason to lie and the lack of supporting evidence.

2. Laura **P**—is a primary source about talking with Jill (but she was not at the scene of the baby-sitting); **R**—may have a reason to lie if she wants to protect Jill (we don't know); **O**—has supporting evidence provided by Connie's and Ellen's statements; **P**—the statement is public, meant to influence Bob. **Overall**, this is fairly good evidence.

3. Christie **P**—is a primary source; **R**—has no reason to lie, as her statement places the blame on herself; **O**—offers no supporting evidence; **P**—it is a public statement. **Overall**, Christie's evidence is strong. [Admitting she had done wrong is unlikely to be a lie, but it is possible—for example, if she had failed because she had skipped school, which might have gotten her into worse trouble.]

Worksheet E: Cause-and-Effect Reasoning

Objectives

To recognize cause-and-effect reasoning
To evaluate cause-and-effect reasoning

Teaching Ideas

INTRODUCING THE SKILL

Introduce cause-and-effect reasoning by telling the class that you, the teacher, just entered the emergency room with a terrible pain in your stomach. They are the doctors on duty. What would they ask? Set it up that you have been at the beach all day and left your ham and mayonnaise sandwich out in the hot sun.

Although some student may focus on what you ate and the likelihood of food poisoning early in the discussion, other students may later ask questions about appendicitis, medication, and alcohol. They are considering other possible causes for the problem. You could ask the class how they could test their hypothesis further to focus them on the connection between each proposed cause and effect. How could they check to be more certain it was food poisoning from the sandwich? (A blood test showing bacteria in the blood would show a connection).

REINFORCING THE SKILL

While these questions for evaluating cause-and-effect reasoning are being discussed, write them on the chalkboard. As with evaluating evidence, the students should be instructed to copy the questions into their notebooks and someone should make a poster to be put up in the classroom. For further discussion of this skill, refer students to the **Cause-and-Effect Reasoning** section of the "Guide to Critical Thinking" (pp. 5–7 in their text).

USING THE WORKSHEET

Once you have laid out the steps in evaluating cause-and-effect reasoning you can pass out Worksheet E for students to try for guided practice. When they have completed the worksheet, have them compare answers in small groups or in a whole-class discussion.

Suggested Answers

1.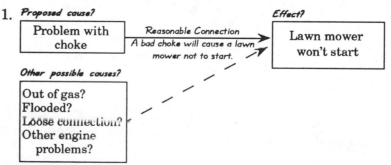

Overall, this is not very strong reasoning since other possible causes have not been ruled out.

2.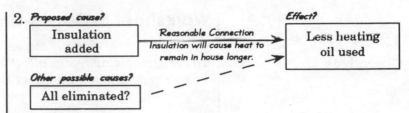

Proposed cause?

Insulation added

Reasonable Connection Insulation will cause heat to remain in house longer.

Effect?

Less heating oil used

Other possible causes?

All eliminated?

Overall, this is very strong reasoning since other possible causes have been ruled out.

3.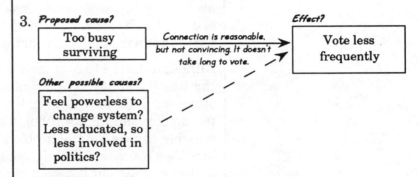

Proposed cause?

Too busy surviving

Connection is reasonable, but not convincing. It doesn't take long to vote.

Effect?

Vote less frequently

Other possible causes?

Feel powerless to change system? Less educated, so less involved in politics?

Overall, the other possible causes seem as important to the effect as the proposed cause. It is not a very strong argument.

Worksheet F: Comparison Arguments

Objectives

To introduce criteria for evaluating comparisons

Teaching Ideas

INTRODUCING THE SKILL

Have students do the introductory problem first. Make sure they write down their questions, then discuss the problem as a class.

After they have given their answers to the autocross problem, ask students what questions they ask to evaluate comparisons in general? (How are the two cases different?) If necessary, refer students to the section on **Comparisons** in the "Guide to Critical Thinking" (pp. 7–8 in the student text).

USING THE WORKSHEET

When students are ready to evaluate the comparison arguments, have them write their answers individually, then discuss the problems in small groups. Note to students that in Problem 3, since Candice is arguing that the radios are different, the students should focus on identifying similarities.

Suggested Answers

INTRODUCTORY PROBLEM

Some Autocross Race questions to ask:

1. What kind of car were you driving?
2. Was it the same course?
3. What were the weather conditions?

Emphasize to the students that they already know how to evaluate comparison arguments. They just showed it by the questions they asked.

COMPARISONS

1. Margarine substitute

   — Compared: butter and margarine

   — Possible differences: taste; amount or type of fat

   — Possible similarities: function in baking

   — Overall: They are similar enough to allow the cake to still come out as a cake, although there might be some difference in taste and texture. To demonstrate the similarities between butter and margarine, ask students what would happen if they substituted jelly for butter.

2. Statewide test

   — Compared: student performance on one test at Centralville and Evantown

— Possible differences:

a. The student body of the two schools might be very different. For example, students might vary in educational background, ethnic background, economic opportunities, or social class.

b. The test may have been given in different grades in the two schools.

c. The curriculum at Centralville might be more suited to the test.

d. Testing circumstances at the two schools may have differed; e.g., physical testing environment; attitudes of students toward test; school activities before or after test, etc.

—Possible similarities: All above items might be similar rather than different.

—Overall: Not enough information is given. If most or all of the above items are different, then the comparison is very weak.

3. Deluxe Radio

—Compared: deluxe and standard radio models

—Possible differences: Cost is the only known difference; number of stations and sound quality are implied differences.

—Possible similarities: We don't know if the standard radio can also do the things the deluxe model can do.

—Overall: Candice has not drawn a reasonable conclusion. She may be satisfied with the radio, but she has not shown that the extra $50 was worth it. If the standard radio plays all the stations she likes and has a clear sound, then Candice's money was not well spent. In this comparison, the possible similarities undermine the argument because Candice is arguing they are different and that the difference makes the extra money spent worthwhile.

Worksheet G: Understanding Comparisons

Objectives

To identify comparison reasoning
To evaluate comparison arguments

Teaching Ideas

Have students write their answers individually, then discuss and defend their answers in small groups. Or you can discuss answers as a class.

Suggested Answers

• Numbers 1 and 5 are comparisons. Other items may have comparisons implied in them, but the comparison is not a key part of the argument.

8. A	11. D	14. D
9. D	12. A	
10. D	13. A	

15. a. Compares John's taste in movies to mine.

   b. It's an alike comparison.

   c. Since John is different from me in some ways, his taste in movies is likely to be different from mine in some ways.

   d. If John's movie taste is different from mine in a way that's important for this movie, then it might be a poor comparison. For example, if John doesn't mind violence in movies but I do, and if this movie is violent, then the comparison argument is faulty.

16. a. Compares Wranglers' team record to Panthers' team record.

   b. It's a different comparison (claims that since they are different from each other in a particular way, they are different in other particular ways also).

   c. Additional information would be needed in the areas of number of games and opponents. They may be similar or different.

   d. The more similarities that are found between the two teams, the stronger the argument that the Wranglers' team is better.

17. a. Compares state university to private college.

   b. It's an alike comparison.

c. Areas of possible comparison might include social life, facilities, library sources, cost, etc.

d. Maybe other aspects of the private college are better. On the other hand, if the campus and professors are the most important considerations to Carrie, then this is a good comparison.

18. a. Compares the private college to public colleges. (The comparison is implicit in "extra money.")

b. It is a difference comparison.

c–d. Since the statement doesn't say that the soccer team and the professors are better than at other, less expensive schools, there is no basis for making the claim that the extra money was worth it.

Worksheet H: Evaluating Generalizations

Objectives

To recognize and evaluate generalizations

Teaching Ideas
USING THE WORKSHEET

The first worksheet section focuses on evaluating generalization claims. A circle diagram is shown for the example problem. If students find such diagrams helpful, encourage them to draw their own for problems 1–3.

The second section of the worksheet focuses on how far given information may be generalized. There is room for reasonable disagreement on these questions, so try to avoid pushing for one right answer. Ask students for the reasons for their answers. Focus on the subgroups of the major group in the generalization.

You might want to have the class read over the section on generalizations in the "Guide to Critical Thinking." If not, you can refer them to that section if they need help.

Suggested Answers

1. a. The generalization is that most kids in the school watch more than 12 hours of television a week.

   b. Subgroups might include honors, average, or remedial students; those involved in extracurricular activities and those who aren't; students who have jobs and those who don't; students from various income levels; students of various home environments; and so forth.

   c. The sample is relatively small (30 out of 800, or about 4%).

   d. The sample may have most of the subgroups by random distribution, but since it is a specific class, it is an ability group.

   e. This isn't a great sample because the amount of homework generally affects how much television a student watches. If this is a remedial class, the number of hours watched probably is not the same as the number of hours watched by honors students.

2. a. The generalization is that all Italians belong to the Mafia.

   b. Subgroups include different intelligence levels; different levels of education, income, and occupation; different geographic locations; different family lives and background; and so forth.

c. The sample may be exceedingly small (this person may know one Italian who belongs to the Mafia), somewhat larger (the person may live in an Italian neighborhood and know many Italians), or nonexistent (the person may have heard that Italians belong to the Mafia). Even with the larger sample, however, it is very small compared to the millions of Italians in the world.

d. We don't know much about the sample, but we can say with reasonable assurance that not all the subgroups are represented well.

e. This is a poor generalization. It is a good example of a stereotype—a large, complex group of people being simplified to all having a particular characteristic.

3. a. The generalization is that the population of Mudville rose dramatically in the 1970s.

b. As far as we know, the sample covers everyone in the large group (Mudville).

c. The generalization is very strong, which tells us that census records are good sources.

4. Neither A nor D are reasonable extensions of the information in your sample since both contain nonpublic, nonsuburban, and nonsecondary schools. (Is homework a key to good grades in elementary schools?) B, although restricted to your own suburban district, is weak for one of the same reasons that A and D are weak: it includes elementary schools. C is the best of the given choices. It is restricted to public suburban high schools, although it does extend the sample generalization too far geographically.

5. D is the best choice since it is the only one that emphasizes both the mountains and a strong defense. A emphasizes only defense, and it is unclear how being large or small affects avoiding war (B and C).

6. A is the best choice. The students in your school may be different (for example, in terms of educational or cultural background) from those in other schools, which makes it difficult to extend the sample beyond your own school (B and C). The information you have says nothing about the type of music students do not like.

Worksheet I: Identifying Unstated Assumptions—1

Objectives

To recognize arguments based on assumptions
To identify assumptions made by others

Teaching Ideas

INTRODUCING THE SKILL

To encourage students to begin recognizing their own assumptions, give half the class statement 1 and the other half statement 2. Ask them to write an answer to the question. Don't say they have different statements.

1. "The Soviet Union gives a great deal of economic aid to India." Why do you think the Soviet Union does this?

2. "The United States gives a great deal of economic aid to India." Why do you think the United States does this?

When each student has written a response, list the various reasons on the chalkboard and ask the students to count the number of positive and negative motives attributed to each country. Were more positive motives given to the United States? If so, why?

Students may contend that the Soviet Union is an expansionist country which is trying to spread communism. The question "How do you know they are expansionist?" will force them to examine how they arrived at their belief. Similarly, "How do you know the United States is giving aid for humanitarian reasons?" will force them to question how they arrived at that belief. While it *may* be true that Soviet aid is self-serving and American aid is humanitarian, students should examine how they arrived at these beliefs. Did they have supporting evidence or did their frame of reference lead to the assumption?

USING THE WORKSHEET

It is probably better to start with this worksheet rather than Worksheet J. If students can identify the assumptions on this worksheet, then they probably do not need the more structured approach.

Suggested Answers

1. Your brother gets good grades in school because he studies. Your lower grades in school are due to lack of study (as opposed to other reasons).

2. Peter is the same age as (or older than) Marie.

3. You run faster than I do.

4. You don't have good writing skills.

5. I don't have other unexpected expenses. I'll be alive. I'll be able to drive.

6. Drinking is a way to enjoy life. Jim is too serious.

Worksheet J: Identifying Unstated Assumptions—2

Objectives

To provide a structured approach to identifying assumptions in arguments

Teaching Ideas

It is probably a good idea to start assumptions with Introductory Worksheet I. If students can identify the assumptions in that worksheet, then they may not need this more structured approach. You may also choose to use this step-by-step approach with only a few students.

If you do use this worksheet, have the students discuss problem 1 as a class before they go on. Give students time to do problem 2 individually, then discuss their answers. Repeat this procedure for problem 3.

Suggested Answers

2. Step 1: (Premise) "Because" Fred works for a station which does fine work...

   Step 2: (Conclusion) "Therefore," Fred is a good mechanic.

   Step 3: (Unique parts) works for a station which does fine work/good mechanic

   Step 4: (Assumption) "People" who work for a station which does fine mechanical work must be good mechanics.

3. Step 1: (Premise) "Because" Sequoia is in the band (and Leona isn't)...

   Step 2: (Conclusion) "Therefore," Sequoia is a better musician (than Leona).

   Step 3: (Unique parts) in the band/better musician

   Step 4: (Assumption) "People" who are in a band are better musicians (than those who aren't).

WORKSHEET A   The Bermuda Triangle

(1) The Bermuda Triangle—an area roughly from Bermuda, southwest to Florida, then east out into the Atlantic, and then northwest back to Bermuda—is one of the most dangerous and strange spots on earth. Beginning back in the 1600s and continuing to today, the number of ships lost in the Triangle is staggering. In recent years an average of about one hundred ships and many airplanes have been lost in the area each year. It is common knowledge among commercial pilots and ship captains that the Triangle is a dangerous place.

(2) What has happened to these boats and planes is especially mysterious, however, and that is what gives the area its name as the "Devil's Triangle." For example, a boat named the *Hollyhock* was off the coast of Florida when it suddenly lost radio contact with the coast. Later, it picked up California on the radio. Then it spotted land on its monitors where there was no land! The *Hollyhock* disappeared without a trace.

(3) Another boat, the *Witchcraft*, was at Buoy Number 7, only two miles off the coast of Miami, when the owner radioed to the Coast Guard for assistance because the boat was taking on water. He reassured the Coast Guard, however, that the boat was in no serious danger for it had built-in flotation chambers. When the Coast Guard arrived at Buoy Number 7, the *Witchcraft* had vanished.

(4) Airplanes, too, have had bizarre incidents. The *Star Tiger*, flying over the Devil's Triangle, suddenly lost all radio contact. No wreckage of the plane was ever found. In 1963 two KC-135 jet tankers disappeared three hundred miles southwest of Bermuda. What caused these planes to go down?

(5) Probably the most incredible incident concerned Training Flight 19, which took off from Fort Lauderdale, Florida, on December 5, 1945. Five Avenger aircraft took off that day on a regular Navy training flight. Pilot Cosner did not go on the flight. Why not? Commander Taylor also seemed hesitant. Did he have the same peculiar feeling as Cosner? The flight was routine at first, but then mysterious things started to happen. The pilots seemed confused and their instruments were doing weird things. The air base which had radio contact with the planes heard the pilots say, "Which way is west?" and the phrases "upside down" and "white water." The planes kept changing directions, almost flying in circles. Then—silence. A search plane was sent out and it, too, disappeared. The Navy has kept the incident quiet, and it hasn't denied the stories that authors have written about it.

(6) It is difficult to explain what happens in the Devil's Triangle. Some people believe there is a magnetic field which throws everything off. Others believe it has to do with the lost continent of Atlantis. Whatever the cause, it is worth thinking twice before traveling through this area—one of the strangest spots on our earth.

Relevant Information on the Bermuda Triangle

1. The *Star Tiger*'s flight was at night in poor weather.

2. It is not unheard of, although it is infrequent, for boats out in the ocean to pick up distant areas on the radio.

3. Rain clouds can sometimes look like land on radar.

4. The *Witchcraft* was out in bad weather.

5. Coast Guard reports make no mention of the *Witchcraft* being near Buoy Number 7. An author estimated the location by comparing several reports.

6. It would have taken the Coast Guard about twenty minutes to get from their station to where the *Witchcraft* was.

7. In twenty minutes a boat in calm seas can drift about one mile.

8. It is extremely difficult to find the wreckage of a plane or boat in the ocean, even on a clear day.

9. Debris found in one spot in the ocean contained the serial numbers of both KC-135 jet tankers. Some observers say this indicates that the two planes collided in the air.

10. The editor of *Aviation Week* stated that, based on a statistical analysis of the number of accidents in an area compared with the number of flights in that area, the Bermuda Triangle is one of the safest spots in the world. It is a popular area with pilots.

11. An Avenger aircraft will sink into the ocean roughly forty-five seconds after splashing down.

12. Two of the men who were in the radio tower in Fort Lauderdale at the time of Training Flight 19 do not recall the Avenger pilots saying "Which way is west?" or "upside down" or "white water." These two men say the planes were definitely lost.

13. Commander Taylor of Training Flight 19 radioed, "If we fly north, then east, we'll get home." He also mentioned being over the Keys (islands). He may have thought he was over the Florida Keys, when actually he was over the Grand Keys in the Atlantic. His proposed course of "north, then east" would have taken the planes toward the middle of the Atlantic.

14. At the time that radio contact was lost with the plane sent to search for Training Flight 19, people on the coast saw what looked like an explosion near the search plane's last-reported location.

15. Out of 10,000 distress calls made to the Coast Guard in that area, about 100 ships are lost in the Bermuda Triangle each year.

16. According to the Coast Guard, many pleasure boat owners don't know what they're doing in the ocean. For example, when the Coast Guard told one owner to plot a course toward an island, the owner said he couldn't find it on his map. The Coast Guard asked him what map he was using, and he said he was looking at the world atlas.

17. Each author who writes about the Bermuda Triangle describes a triangle of a different size and shape from the other authors.

18. The author of this Bermuda Triangle article writes books on popular subjects, such as mysterious and bizarre phenomena.

WORKSHEET B   Evaluating Evidence

Background

You, as a historian, are trying to decide who stabbed John Jones in 1940 in the corridor at your school. You have gathered the following information (evidence) about the case.

Relevant Information

A.   The report on the police investigation into the death of John Jones says:

1. The police concluded that he was murdered by stab wounds.
2. The police had three suspects: 1) Kid Kelly, 2) Slim Stowell, and 3) Lucky Levin. All three were in the corridor within ten feet of Jones when he was murdered.
3. Police thought they had enough evidence to prosecute Lucky Levin.

B.   Lucky Levin was tried for the alleged murder of John Jones. In the trial:

4. Lucky's girlfriend said he was a good person and would never kill anyone.
5. A teacher testified he opened the door of his room and entered the corridor as soon as he heard John Jones scream. No one could have moved, and no one was moving when he looked into the corridor. Jones was lying on the floor while Lucky, Kid, and Slim were standing within ten feet, looking at him. Lucky was closest to Jones.
6. Kid testified that he didn't do it, but he was looking the other way so he doesn't know whether Lucky or Slim did it.
7. Slim testified that he didn't do it, Lucky did it.
8. Lucky testified that he didn't do it, Slim did it.
9. Witness A, who didn't know any of the men, said he heard Jones say, "No, Lucky, no" right before the murder.
10. Witness B, who was 35 feet away and who didn't know any of the men, said he saw Lucky stab Jones.
11. The knife was shown to have Lucky's, and only Lucky's, fingerprints on it.
12. According to Kid, both Lucky and Slim had knives with them on the day of the death.
13. The police found a knife on Slim at the scene of the murder, as well as the knife in Jones. No other weapons were found.
14. An IOU note produced at the trial showed that Jones owed Lucky $300, which had been due to be paid three days before the murder.
15. Witness C testified that Slim did not like Jones.
16. Witness D, 50 feet away, testified that she saw Lucky stab Jones.
17. Witness E, in another part of the building and not within sight of the murder scene, says he's sure Lucky killed Jones.
18. At the trial, a letter from Lucky's girlfriend to her mother was introduced as evidence. The letter said that Lucky hated John Jones.

C.   The jury found Lucky guilty of murder.

Evaluate the Evidence

Q As a historian, do you think the jury was right in its verdict? Why do you think so?

Q Give one example from the Relevant Information section on page 33 for each type of evidence listed below. Write the number of the evidence on the line provided.

_____A. Statements by witnesses

_____B. Documents (written information)

_____C. Objects

Q Evaluate (judge) the following evidence selected from the Relevant Information. Use the **PROP** factors (criteria) from the section on **Evidence** in the "Guide to Critical Thinking" (pp. 2–4).

Factor #	4	7	10	11	14	17	18
P							
R							
O							
P							

Q Compare the reliability of evidence 4 and evidence 18. Which is more reliable? Explain your answer.

WORKSHEET C   Sources and Evidence

Whenever you see information used in support of an argument you should ask certain questions, the first and most important being, "Does the information have a source given?"

A *source* is the person, place, or written document the information came from. If there is no given source, the information cannot be evaluated and should not be accepted as reliable.

If the information does give a source, you can evaluate its reliability by asking a number of questions, four of which are given here. For further help, see the section on **Evidence** in the "Guide to Critical Thinking."

Criteria for Evaluating Evidence

P   Is it a **primary** (more reliable) or secondary (less reliable) source?

R   Does the person giving the evidence have any **reason to lie** (less reliable)?

O   Is there **other evidence** which supports or verifies what this evidence says (more reliable) or is this the only evidence presented on the topic (less reliable)?

P   Is it a public (less reliable) or **private** (more reliable) statement? It is public if the person giving it knew other people would **read** or **see** it.

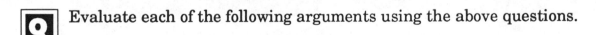 Evaluate each of the following arguments using the above questions.

1.   The city government under Mayor Elwell was very corrupt. Over $15 million was stolen in only five years.

   Is there a source given for any information in this argument? _____
   If not, the claim of corruption is not well supported by evidence.
   If yes, evaluate the evidence and explain your evaluation.

   P

   R

   O

   P

2.   Kurt is a great hitter. The statistics from last season's scorebook show he hit .457, a very high average.

      Is there a source given for any information in this argument? _____

      If not, the argument is not well supported. If yes, evaluate it.

      P

      R

      O

      P

3.   The city government under Mayor Pratt was very corrupt. Three city workers stated in public hearings that they each had seen money paid to city officials for special favors.

      Is there a source given for any information in this argument? _____

      If not, the argument is not well supported. If yes, evaluate it.

      P

      R

      O

      P

4.   Kelley is a great hitter. She can hit the fast ball and the curve.

      Is there a source given for any information in this argument? _____

      If not, the argument is not well supported. If yes, evaluate it.

      P

      R

      O

      P

WORKSHEET D   Evaluating Evidence — PROP

You will recall that the first question you should ask about information (evidence) is whether or not a source is given. Each argument on this worksheet names the source, or the person who said it. For further explanation see the section on **Evidence** in the "Guide to Critical Thinking."

Criteria for Evaluating Evidence

P   Is it a **primary** (more reliable) or secondary (less reliable) source?

R   Does the person giving the evidence have any **reason to lie** (less reliable)?

O   Is there **other evidence** which supports or verifies what this evidence says (more reliable) or is this the only evidence presented on the topic (less reliable)?

P   Is it a public (less reliable) or **private** (more reliable) statement? It is public if the person giving it knew other people would read or see it.

Q   Evaluate each of the following situations according to the four criteria given below.

1.   Yu-chi tells his father it was not his fault that he got detention. He said that the teacher thought he was talking during class, but he wasn't.

     Evaluate Yu-chi's evidence according to the four criteria.

         P

         R

         O

         P

Overall, how reliable is Yu-chi's evidence?

---

2. Bob is angry because he thinks his girlfriend, Jill, went out with Larry on Friday. Laura, Connie, and Ellen all told Bob that they had talked with Jill on the phone most of the night on Friday while she was baby-sitting, so she couldn't have gone out with Larry.

   Evaluate Laura's evidence according to the four criteria.

   P

   R

   O

   P

   Overall, how reliable is Laura's evidence?

3. Christie tells her parents she failed English because she didn't study. She says she has no one to blame but herself and has to admit she deserves to be grounded.

   Evaluate Christie's evidence about why she failed.

   P

   R

   O

   P

   Overall, how reliable is Christie's evidence?

 ©1991 Midwest Publications/Critical Thinking Press and Software, P.O. Box 448, Pacific Grove, CA 93950

WORKSHEET E   Cause-and-Effect Reasoning

When someone proposes a cause for some situation or event, he or she is using cause-and-effect reasoning. Following these steps will help you evaluate such arguments.

EVALUATING CAUSE-AND-EFFECT REASONING

1.   Decide which is the cause and which is the effect.

2.   See if the person explains how the cause led to the effect. If the person doesn't explain, we should ask if there is a reasonable connection between the cause and the effect.

3.   Ask if there are other possible causes for this effect. Has this person eliminated these other possible causes?

Q   Using a diagram like the one shown after the first problem will help you follow these steps when evaluating cause-and-effect reasoning. Draw your own diagrams for the other problems.

1.   The repairman says that Mark's lawn mower won't start because of a problem with the choke, which will cost $25.00 to fix.

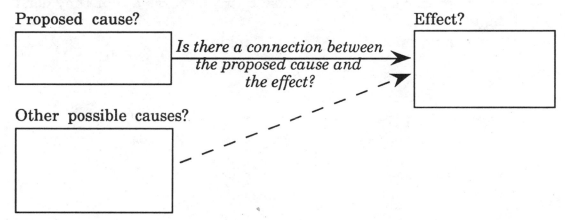

Proposed cause?

Is there a connection between the proposed cause and the effect?

Effect?

Other possible causes?

Overall, how strong is the repairman's cause-and-effect reasoning?

---

2. Mr. Alberti insulated his house before this winter started. The average temperature this winter has been about the same as last winter, and Mr. Alberti has kept the thermostat at the same settings both winters. So far, he has used 40% fewer gallons of oil than he had at this time last winter. He thinks the insulation has been very effective in saving heating oil.

Analyze Mr. Alberti's cause-and-effect thinking. Use a diagram.

Overall, how strong is the argument?

3. Low-income people tend to vote less frequently than high-income people because poorer people are so busy trying to survive that they don't take time to vote.

Draw a diagram and analyze this thinking.

Overall, how strong is the argument?

WORKSHEET F   Comparison Arguments

Introductory Problem

> Suppose you drove in an autocross race at the North Shore Shopping Center parking lot a month ago. ("Autocross" is a race over a winding course set up with cone markers. Cars race one at a time and are clocked as they run the course.) You drove your 1952 Plymouth, and your time was 36.8 seconds. Now, suppose Harry told you that last Sunday he was in an autocross and his time was 28.2 seconds. He says this proves he is a better driver than you are.

Write three questions that you would want to ask Harry.

1.

2.

3.

Evaluating Comparison Arguments

A comparison argument reasons that since two cases are similar in some respects they will also be similar in another way. You can tell from the questions you wrote above that the key to deciding the strength of a comparison argument is asking, "How are the two cases different?" Refer to the section on **Comparison Reasoning** in the "Guide to Critical Thinking" (Unit 1) if you need more help.

 Using the given questions, evaluate each of the following comparison arguments.

1. You are baking a cake and the recipe calls for 5 teaspoons of butter. You have no butter, so you reason that if you substitute 5 teaspoons of margarine the cake will still turn out fine.

    a.   What two items are being compared?

    b.   How are they different?

    c.   How are they alike?

    d.   Overall, how strong is this comparison argument?

2. The average score on the state-wide test was 12 points higher at Centralville High than it was at Evantown High. It is clear from these scores that the teachers at Centralville are doing a better job of teaching.

    a. What two items are being compared?

    b. How are they different?

    c. How are they alike?

    d. Overall, how strong is this comparison argument?

3. Candice paid $50 more to get the deluxe model when she bought her radio. She thinks the money was well spent because the radio gets all the stations she likes and the sound is very clear.

    a. What two items are being compared?

    b. How are they different?

    c. How are they alike?

    d. Overall, how strong is this comparison argument?

WORSHEET G   Understanding Comparisons

For help, refer to the section about **Comparisons** in the "Guide to Critical Thinking."

Identifying Comparisons

Q Put a "C" on the line in front of each of the following arguments or claims that use comparison reasoning.

_____ 1.   Jean felt the suede jacket was worth the extra money.

_____ 2.   Benji has been a great dog. He's very obedient and he doesn't bark much.

_____ 3.   Fred used his new equipment the last time he climbed.

_____ 4.   I decided to read *A Tale of Two Cities* because, although it is long, it is an excellent story.

_____ 5.   You should buy alkaline batteries; they last longer than regular ones.

_____ 6.   Tom and Pat helped us out a lot when we had to fix the house. They are good neighbors.

_____ 7.   Tomika hit the other car when she backed up in the parking lot.

Categorizing Comparisons

Q Mark each of the following arguments. Put an **S** in front of arguments which claim that the two cases are basically similar. Put a **D** in front of arguments which claim that the two cases are basically different. Remember, better/worse comparisons emphasize differences.

_____ 8.   You gave Mari $5.00 for her work, so you should give me $5.00 for my work, too.

_____ 9.   Since our team has won more games this year than last, we must have improved.

_____ 10.   Rachel is the right player to guard their scorer. Julie just isn't as good on defense.

_____ 11.   The new deluxe sedan costs a little more but it's well worth it. It has cruise control and an engine.

_____ 12.   I beat George at chess last time, so I'm sure I will again.

_____ 13.   Jim has never charged us more than $50.00 for a repair in the past, so he surely won't charge us too much this time.

_____ 14.   I'm sticking with Toni because she's a better computer programmer than Geoffrey is.

Analyzing and Evaluating Comparisons

 Each of the following problems presents a comparison argument for you to analyze and evaluate. The **Example** is done for you.

Example:

"I jumped 5'6" in the last meet, so I should jump at least 5'6" today.

    a.   What are the two cases or characteristics being compared?

        Case A: [the speaker's jumping ability at the last meet]

        Case B: [the speaker's jumping ability today]

    b.   Is this an alike or different comparison?

        [Alike]

    c.   What similarities or differences are there between the two cases?

        [Similarities: same goal in same event]

        [Differences: the jumper's health or condition may be different today; weather, jumping conditions, or training time may differ]

    d.   How strong is the comparison?

        [It's reasonable, but it should take into account the possible differences. For example, if the jumper claimed to be in better condition now and the weather is favorable, then the conclusion would be stronger.]

15. "My best friend, John, liked the movie, so I bet I'll like it too."

    a.   What are the two cases or characteristics being compared? Be precise!

        Case A:

        Case B:

    b.   Is this an alike or different comparison?

    c.   What similarities or differences are there between the two cases?

    d.   How strong is the comparison?

16. "The Wranglers have a better team than the Panthers. The Wranglers have more wins and fewer losses."

    a.   What are the two cases or characteristics being compared?

        Case A:

        Case B:

    b.   Is this an alike or different comparison?

c.   What similarities or differences are there between the two cases?

d.   How strong is the comparison?

17. Carrie decided that the state university is just as good as the private college in her area. The campus and the professors at the state university are as good as those at the private college.

a.   What are the two cases or characteristics being compared?

Case A:

Case B:

b.   Is this an alike or different comparison?

c.   What similarities or differences are there between the two cases?

d.   How strong is the comparison?

18. Roger decides that the extra money he spends to attend the private college is well worth it. The soccer team is excellent at the private college, as are the professors.

a.   What are the two cases or characteristics being compared?

Case A:

Case B:

b.   Is this an alike or different comparison?

c.   What similarities or differences are there between the two cases?

d.   How strong is the comparison?

WORSHEET H   Evaluating Generalizations (Samples)

If you need help, refer to the definition and examples of **Generalization** in the "Guide to Critical Thinking." Remember that a circle diagram is useful to help visualize generalizations as an analysis aid. An example is done for you.

Example:

"Most American adults would like to own their own homes. Just last month a survey of 1232 students at five hundred colleges around the country showed that 62% of those students who responded want to own their own home."

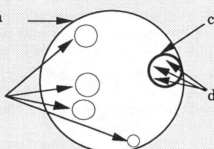

a. What generalization is being made about the whole group?

c. How large is the sample?

b. What subgroups make up the whole group?

d. Does the sample have all the same subgroups in the same proportion as the whole group?

  a. Generalization?
      [Most American adults want to own homes.]

  b. Subgroups of whole group?
      [Subgroups include men and women and various geographic regions, ages, incomes, and levels of education.]

  c. Size of sample?
      [The sample is rather small, compared to the number of people in the whole group, so representativeness will be important.]

  d. Representativeness of sample?
      [The sample includes men and women (probably) from different geographic regions, but is not representative in any other way. The sample consists of people who are young, have a relatively high level of income, and have a uniformly high level of education.]

  e. Overall, how strong is the generalization?
      [This is a very weak sample; therefore, it is not a good generalization.]

Q Evaluate the following generalizations. Draw a circle graph and use the given questions to help with your evaluation.

1. "Most students in this high school [800 students] watch more than twelve hours of television a week. We took a poll in my social studies class, and twenty out of the thirty students said they watch more than twelve hours a week." [This school has honors, average, and remedial classes.]

    a. Generalization?

    b. Subgroups of whole group?

    c. Size of sample?

    d. Representativeness of sample?

    e. Strength of generalization?

2. "I wouldn't hire an Italian if I were you. They all belong to the Mafia. Pretty soon you'll start having problems."
    a. Generalization?

    b. Subgroups of whole group?

    c. Size of sample?

    d. Representativeness of sample?

    e. Strength of generalization?

3. "The 1980 census [a survey of every household in the country] showed that the population of Mudville rose dramatically during the 1970s."
    a. Generalization?

    b. Subgroups of whole group?

    c. Size of sample?

    d. Representativeness of sample?

    e. Strength of generalization?

Write the letter of the most reasonable generalization on the line in front of each item. Explain your choice in the space provided.

_____4. Suppose you found that in your public, suburban high school, those students who do more homework also get better grades. Which of the following is the best generalization to make from this information?

    A. In your state, students who do more homework get better grades.

    B. In your school district, students who do more homework get better grades.

    C. In public, suburban high schools in the United States, students who do more homework get better grades.

    D. Students who do more homework get better grades.

Explain your choice.

_____5. Suppose you knew that Switzerland, which is a small, mountainous country, has used a strong defense (large military) to successfully avoid war. Which of the following is the best generalization to make from this information?

    A. A large military is the key to avoiding war.

    B. Small countries can use a strong defense to avoid war.

    C. Large countries can use a strong defense to avoid war.

    D. Mountainous countries can avoid war through building a strong defense.

Explain your choice.

_____6. You know that 75% of the kids in your ninth-grade homeroom like rock music best. Which of the following is the best generalization to make from this information?

    A. Most ninth-graders in your school like rock music best.

    B. Anywhere you go in the country, you'll find that most teenagers like rock music best.

    C. All ninth-grade students like rock music best.

    D. Few ninth-grade students in your school like classical music.

Explain your choice.

WORKSHEET I   Identifying Unstated Assumptions — 1

What are the unstated assumptions in each of the following arguments? If you need help, look at the section on **Assumptions** in the "Guide to Critical Thinking."

1. "Why can't you study like your brother? He gets all A's in school."

2. "Beth is older than Peter, so she must be older than Marie also."

3. "Even if I have a head start running to the beach, you'll get there first."

4. "Are you sure you want to apply for that job? It requires someone with good writing skills."

5. "When I get my raise, I'm going to buy a new car."

6. "Jim, why don't you come drinking with us? You've got to learn to relax and enjoy life."

WORSHEET J   Identifying Unstated Assumptions — 2

This four-step approach is one method for identifying unstated assumptions.

Step 1	Write out the premise. (The premise is the part of an argument that tells "why" something is true. Look for the place to put "because." What follows is the premise.)
Step 2	Find and write out the conclusion of the argument. (Look for the place to put "therefore." What follows it is the conclusion.)
Step 3	Find the unique part of the conclusion (the part that doesn't appear in the premise) and the unique part of the premise (the part that doesn't appear in the conclusion.)
Step 4	Combine the two unique parts in a sentence that starts with a general word, such as people, wars, or countries. This sentence is the unstated assumption.

 Try the four-step approach on the following claims. If you need help, look at the section on **Assumptions** in the "Guide to Critical Thinking." The first one is done for you as an example.

1. "Roger is not a football player since he weighs only 130 pounds."
    Step 1:   "Because" he weighs only 130 pounds. (Premise)
    Step 2:   "Therefore" Roger is not a football player. (Conclusion)
    Step 3:   ...weighs only 130 pounds (P)/...not a football player (C)
    Step 4:   "People" who weigh only 130 pounds are not football players.

2. Fred is definitely a good mechanic. He works for the service station on Main Street which is known for its fine mechanical work.

    Step 1:

    Step 2:

    Step 3:

    Step 4:

3. Sequoia is in the band and Leona isn't, so Sequoia must be a better musician.

    Step 1:

    Step 2:

    Step 3:

    Step 4:

WORSHEET K   Analyzing Historical Films

When watching a film or video interpretation of any event, consider using the following (**PIPER**) model of analysis.

P	Point of View?
I	Inferences?
P	Persuasive Techniques?
E	Evidence?
R	Relevant Information?

Use this worksheet to help you analyze historical films you watch.

1.   Name of film:

2.   Main point of the film:

3.   **P** What is the **point of view** of the film? Was it overly favorable or critical of a particular group or individual?

4.   **I** What **inferences** were made in the film? Were there parts of the film that the filmmakers must have made up because they couldn't have known this from the available evidence?

5.   **P** What techniques are used in the film to **persuade** the audience to the filmmaker's point of view? Note camera angle, music, character portrayal, etc.

6.   **E** What **evidence** is included to support the point of view put forth in the film? What is the source of that evidence? How strong is it?

7.   **R** What **relevant information** do I know? Does it contradict or support the story presented in the film?

8.   Overall, how strong are the historical arguments in this film? Is it historically accurate?

WORKSHEET L   Analyzing Historical Interpretations

Lesson _____   Interpretation _____

 Answer the following questions on each interpretation.

1. What is the main idea of this interpretation?

2. List two or three key points the author(s) use(s) to support the main idea, write any evidence given to support the point, and evaluate the evidence according to the **PROP** questions.

Key Point	Evidence that supports the point	Evaluation of Evidence
1		
2		

3. Identify and analyze one cause-and-effect argument the interpretation makes. Fill in the cause and the effect first, then complete the diagram.

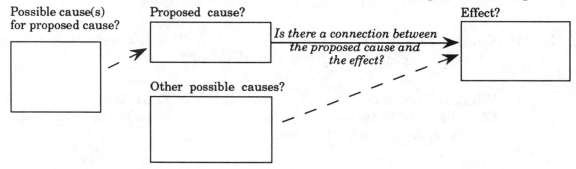

Overall, how strong is this cause-and-effect reasoning?

4. Analyze any other aspect of the argument presented in the interpretation. For example, evaluate a generalization, comparison, or proof argument; identify an unstated assumption; note vague or emotional words that need to be defined more clearly by the author.

5. If **Relevant Information** is provided, does any of the given information affect this interpretation? If so, identify the specific information by number(s) and state the effect(s) of each on the interpretation.

6. What is your overall judgment of the interpretation? Identify its strengths and weaknesses.

UNIT 2
UNITED STATES AS A WORLD POWER

Lesson 1: Identifying and Evaluating Sources

Objectives

To identify sources
To evaluate evidence

Teaching Ideas

This is a basic lesson on identifying when a claim has a source and on evaluating sources. Since the evaluation section is already broken down into subsections (Primary Source, Reason to Lie) this is a relatively easy lesson. If you feel your students do not need so much structure, you could use more challenging lessons on evaluating evidence, such as Lessons 5 and 10, rather than this lesson.

Have the students answer the questions for homework. Then have them compare their answers in pairs or groups of three and finally discuss their answers as a class.

Point out that having a reason to lie does not mean that people are lying. It just means that we cannot rely too much on what they say.

Suggested Answers

IDENTIFYING SOURCES

1. S   Megan and Pedro are the sources.
2. S   The report cards are the sources.
3. N
4. N
5. S   Albert Beveridge is the source.
6. N

PRIMARY SOURCES

7. S   Bob apparently has not seen the new student play.
8. S   Rachel has not seen the movie.
9. S   The publication date, at least 63 years after the event, indicates that La Feber was not there at the time.
10. P   McKinley is reporting on himself. He is always present with himself.
11. P   Wilson—same as #10
12. S   The publication date makes it unlikely that Bailey was present to observe the events of 1914 and 1915.

REASON TO LIE

13. N   Linda is not protecting herself when she confesses.

REASON TO LIE

14. N The pipe cannot lie, it is not alive.

15. N Bryan may have some other reason for opposing imperialism but it is very hard to think of one.

16. R Wilson has reason to say we are fighting for noble purposes. He is unlikely to say, for example, we are fighting to make money or protect loans.

17. N Since the Germans are communicating secretly, they have no reason to lie. This note was intercepted and became public, which very much hurt the Germans.

18. N It is hard to think of a reason why a historian would consciously lie, although historians, like everyone else, are susceptible to biases.

Lesson 2: Evaluating Evidence

Objectives

To evaluate evidence

Teaching Ideas

This is a more advanced lesson on evaluating evidence than Lesson 1. In this lesson, students must remember the criteria (PROP) in order to evaluate the sources effectively. You might want to do the first problem as a class, have students do the rest of the problems in groups of three, then discuss these problems as a class.

Suggested Answers

EVALUATE THE SOURCES

STRENGTHS

1. [secret cable—Roosevelt to Dewey]

    • It is private (P) so there seems to be no reason to lie (R). Roosevelt is a primary (P) source.

WEAKNESSES

    • There is no other (O) evidence showing an interest in the Philippines as a motive for war with Spain. How do we know that any other American leaders wanted the Philippines?

SUMMARY

    • Overall, this is strong evidence, but evidence is needed to show that other leaders also had an interest in the Philippines.

2. [John Blum]

STRENGTHS

    • There does not seem to be a reason to lie (R).

WEAKNESSES

    • There is no other (O) supporting evidence and it is not a primary source (P).

SUMMARY

    • Overall, this is weak evidence because it is a secondary source.

3. [secret note—Lansing to Wilson]

STRENGTHS

    • It is private (P); Lansing has no reason to lie (R); and it is a primary source (P).

WEAKNESSES

    • There is no other (O) evidence that economic interests pushed the United States to enter World War I.

SUMMARY

    • Overall, this is strong evidence but more is needed.

CHOOSE THE MOST
RELIABLE EVIDENCE

4. D is probably strongest because it is primary (P) and private (P) so Wilson had no obvious reason to lie (R). A is public, B is not by the decision-maker himself, and C does not give reasons for the decision to enter World War I.

5. B is probably strongest because it is primary (P) and private (P). A is public; C and D are secondary sources in terms of the actual decision.

Lesson 3: Determining Causes and Effects

Objectives

To identify cause-and-effect reasoning

Teaching Ideas

Have students do problem 1 and discuss it as a class. Then have them do problems 2–6 and compare answers in small groups. Students can continue by answering the second half of the lesson (problems 7–9) and comparing answers in their groups. All the problems can then be discussed as a class.

The point of the second half of the lesson is to get students to begin generating their own list of causes before accepting other people's proposed causes as the only possible ones.

Suggested Answers
LABEL EACH ITEM

1. C CAUSE: sea power
   EFFECT: nations are great

2. C CAUSE: wanted to make Hawaii part of the United States
   EFFECT: overthrew the Queen

3. N No cause for why he wanted these things is proposed.

4. C CAUSE: war
   EFFECT: cost $250 million

5. N No causes or effects are mentioned.

6. N No causes or effects are proposed.

THINK OF AS MANY
CAUSES AS YOU CAN

7. Attractiveness

   Students should recognize a number of reasons for attractiveness other than jeans, such as, personality, cleanliness, shape, hair, and so forth.

8. Negotiated settlement

   Students should note other reasons for negotiating a settlement, such as raising the leader's prestige in the world or at home, belief in peace, increased trade, and so forth.

9. Defender's advantage

   It is interesting to see what students suggest. A focus is certainly on technology, so the machine gun is probably a big factor.

Lesson 4: Assessing Cause-and-Effect Reasoning

Objectives

To assess cause-and-effect reasoning

Teaching Ideas

Make sure that students understand the factual aspects leading up to the Spanish-American War before they read the historians' viewpoints. It is easy to confuse the revolt in Cuba with the war itself. Also, if students have read about the yellow press before this lesson, they are much more likely to understand what they read here.

Have students answer the questions in writing and then compare answers in small groups and discuss as a class.

Suggested Answers

CONNECTION

1. Which argument is strongest?

   Based on the criterion of connecting the yellow press (the proposed cause) to the decision for war (the effect), the best answer is B. This argument shows that the papers may have distorted the situation in Cuba, that the papers influenced millions of Americans, and that this public opinion, since an election was in progress, influenced American leaders. This is the only argument which shows why the leaders (decision makers) would have been influenced by public opinion. This argument is certainly not strong, since it lacks evidence for two of its premises, and since the evidence it does present is suspect. (Hearst might have exaggerated his role in shaping events to make himself look good.) But B's argument is nevertheless stronger than the other two.

   Historian A gives a good explanation for why newspapers competed, but fails to explain the number of people that were influenced, or to show how public opinion influenced the decision makers. Historian C gives evidence of alleged newspaper exaggerations, but again does not connect the exaggerations to the decision for war.

EVALUATING CAUSE AND
EFFECT

2. **Second, part-time job**

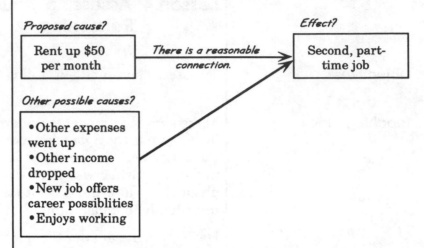

Overall, this argument is reasonable, but there are a number of other possible reasons that she got a second job.

3. **Panama Canal**

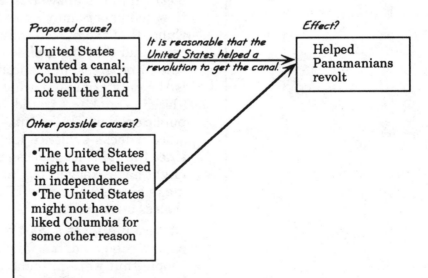

Overall, this argument seems fairly strong in terms of cause-and-effect reasoning. If we did help the revolutionists right after Colombia refused to agree to the canal, then the connection seems quite likely. It is difficult to think of another cause that is as likely. The argument needs evidence to support its premises.

4. Boxer Rebellion

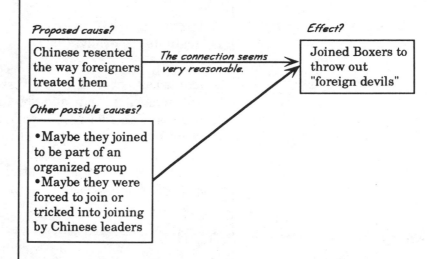

Proposed cause?

Chinese resented the way foreigners treated them

The connection seems very reasonable.

Effect?

Joined Boxers to throw out "foreign devils"

Other possible causes?

• Maybe they joined to be part of an organized group
• Maybe they were forced to join or tricked into joining by Chinese leaders

Overall, this argument appears strong in terms of cause-and-effect reasoning. It seems very logical that people who join an anti-foreigner group probably resent foreigners. Undoubtedly, some people joined for other reasons, but most of them probably joined because of resentment.

Lesson 5: Analyzing Generalizations

Objectives

To identify generalizations
To evaluate generalizations

Teaching Ideas

Students can write their answers for the section on identifying generalizations and you can discuss them quickly as a class. The section on evaluating generalizations is more difficult. It might be best to do problem 6 as a class and then have students do the rest of the problems. It is important to stress that the students should consider the subgroups of the whole population.

Suggested Answers

IDENTIFYING
GENERALIZATIONS

1. N

2. G The cue words "not any" are the negative way of saying "All of the males are not cheerleaders."

3. G "Everyone" is the cue word.

4. G "Most" is the cue word.

5. N

EVALUATING
GENERALIZATIONS

6. Dress shirt and tie to school

This is most likely an informal survey, based on observation rather than statistical sampling. How does the person know, without a survey, that all the boys wearing dress shirts and ties are on athletic teams?

7. Judge popularity

This survey raises the question of randomness as a method of achieving representativeness. Some social scientists believe randomness is the best method for achieving representativeness in sampling, better than any conscious method. We would have to know more about the survey to evaluate it: the region, male-female makeup, income breakdown, etc. It seems reasonable to conclude from the survey, however, that Judge Wapner is more well known than Judge Rehnquist.

8. American opposition to expansion

This is a summary of a point made in a high school history textbook. It is difficult to evaluate it without knowing what kind of evidence indicates many Americans were saddened. Was a survey done at the time? Is it based on protests? Letters to the editor? The argument is also hard to pin down because of the elusive word "many." How many is many?

9. 1916 election

The popular vote statistics are rounded off, but otherwise this is a very accurate statement about the voters since all the votes are counted. The sample takes in the whole population (everyone who voted).

Lesson 6: Why Did President McKinley Ask for a Declaration of War against Spain in April 1898?

Objectives

To find the main idea
To recognize unstated assumptions
To assess cause and effect
To evaluate generalizations
To evaluate proof reasoning
To evaluate comparisons
To evaluate evidence

Teaching Ideas

It is probably best to have students read about the causes of the Spanish-American War before they start this lesson. Ask students what the causes of the Spanish-American War were and list them on the board. Then ask the class what role President McKinley played in the declaration of war. Tell them that McKinley's role is the focus of this lesson.

There are a number of options for using the viewpoints. First, you could have the students read both viewpoints, fill in the worksheet, and then discuss their answers as a class. Second, you could have the class debate why McKinley asked for a declaration of war, based on the viewpoints and outside research. Third, you could have the students evaluate the viewpoints according to the ARMEAR model in the "Guide to Critical Thinking," p. 18. Fourth, you could have the students read the viewpoints without the worksheet and the class could discuss which argument is stronger and why.

You could help students by demonstrating 3a and 7a for them. Once they see how you do it, they will more likely be able to fill in the rest of the items. You can adapt the lesson for less able students by having students fill in only questions 1, 4, 5, 8, and 9 from the worksheet.

Suggested Answers
  HISTORIAN A

1. C

2. Unstated assumption in paragraph 2 (one possible answer):

    The expansionists were important advisers to President McKinley—they really influenced the President.

HISTORIAN A

3. Reasoning

	Type of Reasoning	Key Question	How Well Answered
a.	Primarily Cause and Effect	Is the connection between the cause and the effect shown?	The author does explain that Cuba was dependent upon sugar exports, so some connection is shown.
b.	Cause and Effect	Is the connection shown?	The connection of the yellow press to public opinion in general is not shown, and the connection of public opinion to McKinley's decision for war is weak (endnote 8 is a statement by Lodge—a jingoist—not McKinley).
c.	Sample	Is the sample large or representative enough?	These were New York City newspapers. Did they affect public opinion all over the country? Some historians have argued that they did. This historian needs to deal with the question.
d.	Proof	Does the evidence or argument prove the point?	The evidence is weak, since it is from Lodge, not McKinley. We have *no evidence* that McKinley worried about the fall elections.
e.	Comparison (also Generalization)	Are the two cases sufficiently similar to prove the conclusion?	It may be that Spanish actions were worse than in other cases. Still the analogy sheds some light on the situation.

4. Evidence

a. At first glance, it looks like Hearst would have no reason to distort, since he is admitting dishonesty in his reporting of the Cuban Revolution. On the other hand, Hearst may have been exaggerating his role in bringing about a war which he felt was right.

b. This is strong evidence that de Lôme meant what he said, since he had no obvious reason to distort in a private letter, and the letter made de Lôme look bad. What this evidence shows about the causes of the Spanish-American War is more difficult to decide, however, since it depends upon McKinley's reaction to the de Lôme letter and many other factors.

HISTORIAN B

5. Main point

William McKinley decided on war in 1898 because of Spanish policies regarding Cuba, not because of the yellow press or jingoists.

6. Unstated assumption (Possible answers)

—Leaders are justified in resolving difficulties by war in order to prevent their countries from looking weak.

—Leaders will resort to war to prevent their countries from looking weak.

7. Reasoning

	Type of Reasoning	Key Question	How Well Answered
a.	Debating or Proof	Debating—Does this argument attack the other viewpoint in a fair way?	If the second sentence is correct, this is a very strong argument. This sentence is based, however, on a secondary source (endnote 1) which is not directly related to this topic. (It seems to be talking more about domestic party politics.)
b.	Proof	Does the evidence prove the point?	There is no evidence from McKinley that he felt the difficulties in Cuba were hurting the United States ability to deal with Germany.
c.	Proof (eliminates the *Maine* as an alternative)	Does the argument prove the point?	This argument does not disprove that destruction of the *Maine* was an important cause of the war. There are several possible reasons why the United States waited two months before responding. (For example, McKinley may have been waiting to see if public opinion would die down.) Also there is a probable straw man fallacy (p. 14, "Guide") here, since the other historians say that the *Maine* was one important cause, but not *the* cause.

8. Opinion

   On paper, Spain seems to have agreed to United States demands. The point on Cuban independence is more difficult to decide. In light of the relevant information, Historian B's argument that the United States demands implied Cuban independence is overstated. On the other hand, the Spanish did clearly say to Secretary of State Day that they would not grant Cuban independence.

9. A

   This cartoon emphasizes Spanish brutality and the role of the American press in causing the war. So it tends to support Historian A's viewpoint.

Lesson 7: Why Was the United States Imperialistic from 1890 to 1929?

Objectives

To assess cause and effect
To evaluate generalizations
To evaluate evidence
To evaluate comparisons

Teaching Ideas

This is a difficult lesson as it deals with complex abstract concepts and theories. The introduction explains some of the concepts, but the arguments and theories remain difficult.

You can use the worksheet on the viewpoints or you can have students write out an evaluation of both viewpoints according to the ARMEAR model (p. 18, "Guide to Critical Thinking"). Alternatively, you can have students evaluate the evidence and reasoning in each argument and decide which viewpoint is strongest and why.

You could have the students discuss their evaluations of the two viewpoints in small groups and then discuss them as a class. Or you could have students defend a point of view in a debate and have them research the point of view they are defending.

Evaluations of the two viewpoints will vary greatly from student to student. Students who are experienced at evaluating arguments will raise some significant questions about these viewpoints.

Below are suggested answers for the worksheet followed by a possible analysis with some points that could be raised for discussion.

Suggested Answers

HISTORIAN A

1. Main idea of Historian A—United States imperialism from 1890 to 1929 was caused primarily by declining profits in American businesses. Businesses searched desperately for new markets.

2. Evidence

    a. Endnote 2—Conant is a primary source who has no reason to lie. There is no supporting evidence, however. Also, one person is not a large enough sample to make a generalization about all businessmen.

    b. Endnote 3—This book is a secondary source. Julien

has no apparent reason to lie, but in fact he writes consistently from the Marxist perspective which makes his views slanted by his preconceptions. An interesting question is "Are his views any more biased than non-Marxists?"

3. Evaluate the argument

   a. Paragraph 4—This is a cause and effect argument. The connection between the businessmen seems reasonable, but in fact this historian does not show if the businessmen actually had any influence with McKinley. Thus the direct connection is not shown.

   b. Paragraph 5—There is no evidence to support this argument. It is a cause-and-effect argument. There is a connection between wasting resources and poverty, but there are many other causes for poverty. Also, the foreign companies may actually have increased the standard of living. We really do not know without evidence.

HISTORIAN B

4. Main idea of Historian B—United States imperialism was not due to pressure by American businessmen. You might want to discuss with students the idea of a negative main idea. Are historians who attempt to show the weakness of another theory obligated to replace that theory with their own?

5. Evaluate the evidence

   a. Endnote 1—This is a secondary source which makes it weak. We would like to see primary sources.

   b. Endnote 2—Both of the sources cited are secondary, but at least they support each other in showing that wages in American companies were high.

6. Evaluate the reasoning

   a. Paragraph 2—This is a comparison. The comparison itself looks fine. The investments are both for the same country, using the same currencies during the same years. It is hard to think of differences. Nevertheless, the small amount of foreign investment may have been crucial to business success.

   b. Paragraph 4—It is a cause and effect of sorts. It

argues that since something (B) did not happen then the proposed cause (A) did not happen. The premise that we should see a significant rise in profits may not be correct, however. In fact, maybe just keeping business profits the same was success. Or maybe American businessmen were hoping for increased profits from imperialism but they were disappointed. The question under study is the motive for imperialism, not its outcome.

c. Paragraph 8—This is a cause-and-effect argument in which the author tries to eliminate other possible motives (causes) for building the Panama Canal. This is a reasonably strong argument but it would be stronger with evidence.

OVERALL

7. Students will disagree about which viewpoint is stronger. Make them support their answers.

Suggested Analyses

HISTORIAN A

In paragraph 1 we see a large increase in foreign investment at the same time that the United States became imperialistic (a correlation). The author argues that the increased investments were due to the need by American companies to avoid glutting the American market (the proposed connection between the cause and the effect). If the businessmen really were concerned about declining profits, then they *might* have pushed the United States government to become imperialistic. No evidence is presented, however, to show that government decision makers were influenced by businessmen. Only one businessman (Charles Conant) is presented to support the point that American businessmen, *in general*, feared declining profits. It is also possible that the statistics are a case of special pleading (p. 11, "Guide to Critical Thinking"). The historian may have chosen the most favorable statistics to make his point. We would like to see the figures for the other years and maybe foreign investment as a percentage of GNP or total investments. The students should be asking, "compared to what?"

Historian A does put forth some evidence in endnotes 4 and 5 to show that businessmen tried to influence President McKinley on the Philippines. The quote by Mark Hanna shows that McKinley may have been influenced to take the island for commercial reasons, but the argument would be much better with a quote from McKinley.

No evidence is presented to support the argument about the American Sugar Refining Company (paragraph 3) or the devastating results of United States investments on the Latin American countries (paragraph 5).

HISTORIAN B

In paragraph 2, the author argues that foreign investments were small compared to investments within the country. This is an important point. The foreign investments may, however, have been a critical part of some businesses (averages mask this possibility—it may be the fallacy of composition, p. 10, "Guide to Critical Thinking"). On the other hand, Historian B argues persuasively in paragraph 3 against this exception.

In paragraph 4, Historian B makes a *stated* assumption when he says that we should see profits rise in the United States from 1890 to 1929. There are two possible problems with Historian B's assumption. First, the idea was to keep profits up. The fact that profits did not fall, even though they were low, may show overall success of foreign investment. Second, businessmen may have pushed the United States into imperialistic ventures *hoping* to increase profits, but were unsuccessful in doing so.

The second sentence in paragraph 5 seems weak because capitalist investment in precious metals may have been much larger than in pre-capitalist times.

The argument in paragraph 7 that the American Sugar Refining Company did not profit from American policies in Cuba suffers from the same weakness as was pointed out for the sentence beginning paragraph 4. The fact that the sugar company did not profit does not mean that it did not try to foster imperialistic policies. The drop of sugar imports to the United States from the Dutch West Indies and Europe was beyond the control of the sugar company.

In paragraph 7, one might wonder about the 16% figure—16% of one of the largest sugar crops in the world might be quite significant. Also, Americans may again have been hoping to expand their exports.

The argument on the Panama Canal is quite complex and the author goes into more detail in the original article, ("The Returns to U.S. Imperialism, 1890–1920," *The Journal of Economic History*, XL [June, 1980], pp. 229-52). Students might consider that the canal provided a competitive advantage for American shippers over shippers further from it (those further away would use it less frequently than they would use other routes) or against shippers who used other modes of transportation.

The students should note the general lack of evidence (as opposed to factual information, which is abundant). Also, the sources provided in the endnotes are secondary.

Lesson 8: Who Was Primarily to Blame for the *Lusitania* Tragedy?

Objectives

To identify values and value judgments
To evaluate evidence

Teaching Ideas

One way to begin the lesson is to have students fill in the Value Survey, "Contraband and Submarines" (pp. 54–55). Discussion of this survey has proved to be very interesting and thought provoking. You could use the survey at a later point in the lesson, if desired.

There are a number of different ways to proceed with the lesson. One method is to have students read and evaluate Historian A. Were they convinced by Historian A's argument? If not, what are its weaknesses? Discuss it as a class, then have them repeat the process for Historian B. A second method is to have half the students defend Historian A and half defend Historian B in a debate, either as a class or in several small groups. A third method is to have students evaluate the viewpoints according to the ARMEAR model (p. 18, "Guide to Critical Thinking") and discuss it as a class. A fourth way to do the lesson is to have the students write subquestions to help them break down the topic and compare the two viewpoints. Analyze and discuss the viewpoints as a class according to the subquestions.

Alternative abbreviated viewpoints are provided in this teacher's guide (pp. 73–75) for less able students. These are much shorter and easier to understand than the lengthy interpretations in the student book.

Suggested Analyses

Evaluations of the two viewpoints will vary greatly from student to student. Some of the issues are questions of evidence or reasoning, but many are questions of value positions. For example, is it right to withdraw a ship (the *Juno*) from rescuing survivors when the ship would also be in danger of being sunk? This is why the survey handout is included. Students need to think about their own positions before dealing with the two viewpoints.

One way to break down this complex argument is to ask subquestions on various topics. An analysis of the two viewpoints by subquestions follows:

1. Does the German warning justify torpedoing the ship?

   Obviously a question of value judgment. If you are

forewarned about danger, is the responsibility for your safety your own? Analogies to such issues as cigarette smoking could be used.

2. Was the *Juno* supposed to escort the *Lusitania*?

This is an evidence question and neither historian establishes a convincing case. Historian A's evidence does not clearly show that the *Juno* was supposed to escort the liner, and Historian B argues that a lack of evidence (negative proof fallacy) shows the warship was not ordered to escort the liner. On the other hand, Historian B's argument that the escort by a warship would not have helped the *Lusitania* makes sense.

3. Was the *Lusitania* deliberately left alone to be sunk in order to draw the United States into the war?

Since the *Lusitania* probably was warned (based on the evidence) this line of reasoning seems unlikely. It is interesting that Historian B argues that Winston Churchill's other actions in his life show that he would not deliberately sacrifice people in this way. Tell your students that during World War II Churchill did not warn the city of Coventry that it was going to be bombed by German airplanes because he did not want the Germans to realize that the British had broken their code. Are the two cases similar enough (comparison reasoning) to show that Churchill may have sacrificed the passengers of the *Lusitania* to help draw the United States into the war on Britain's side?

4. Were the Germans forced to sink the *Lusitania* given the circumstances?

A value position question.

5. Was the *Lusitania* sunk primarily by the munitions exploding?

Notice that the two historians agree that the ship was loaded with munitions. Historian B's argument that the small arms ammunition could not have exploded seems strong.

The question of whether the gun cotton or the boilers blew up is more difficult. Historian B's argument that it was illogical to load a ship which the British were hoping to be sunk with needed materials is weak. One group in the British government may have loaded the gun cotton while a separate group in the government may have been setting it up to be sunk. On the other hand, Historian B's argument that it is much more likely that the boilers blew up is strong and is backed by some evidence. Students should ask two questions to help answer this problem:

Does tightly-packed gun cotton (nitrocellulose) really explode on contact with sea water? (Chemists have differing opinions about it.) Where exactly are the holes in the ship? Note that the evidence by the survivors from the boiler rooms does not necessarily rule out the boilers exploding. Historian A only *infers* that because they did not say a boiler blew up that the boilers did not blow up. This is a weak line of reasoning.

6. Did the design of the *Lusitania* mean that the British were partly responsible for the great loss of life?

   This is a value position question. Note that the two historians agree that the ship's design did contribute to the loss of life. They disagree whether the designer bears some responsibility for the disaster.

7. Were the British wrong to recall the *Juno* from rescuing survivors?

   A value position question.

8. Did the British cover up the sinking in their inquiry?

   It seems that the captain of the *Lusitania* was indeed warned of submarine activity in the area, so to that extent it probably was not a cover-up. The questions on munitions, ship's design, etc. may have been covered up, but they may not have been thought to be serious questions. It may have been common knowledge at the time that there was ammunition on board, for example.

ABBREVIATED VIEWPOINT A

Lusitania (A)

—The *Lusitania* was sunk on May 7, 1915, by a German U–boat off the coast of Ireland; 1200 people died.

—The Germans warned the passengers that the ship would be sunk.

—The British did not tell the passengers that the ship was loaded with munitions, nor that gun mounts had been placed on it.

ABBREVIATED VIEWPOINT A

—The British captain told the passengers that the *Lusitania* would be protected by warships, but it was not. The British Admiralty (the leaders of the navy) did not try to protect the ship even though they knew there were submarines in the area.

—The British wanted the United States to come into the war on their side.

—The British figured that if a passenger ship with United States citizens on it was sunk by the Germans, the United States would be very upset. President Wilson had stated that Americans had the right to travel on ships without being harmed.

—The commander of the German U–boat said he fired one torpedo but there were two explosions.

—The *Lusitania* was loaded with gun cotton, which explodes when it comes in contact with salt water.

—The *Lusitania* was designed in a way that caused it to list (tilt to one side) when it was hit. The list prevented most of the lifeboats from being lowered. (See the diagram below.)

—After the *Lusitania* was torpedoed and sunk, rescue ships were sent out. The rescue ships were recalled, however, even though they were within sight of the passengers. During the night most of the passengers drowned.

—Divers stated that the front of the *Lusitania*, where the ammunition and gun cotton were stored, had a huge hole in it, indicating an explosion from inside the ship.

—Two survivors of boiler room 1 and one survivor of boiler room 2 said nothing about boilers exploding. Boiler rooms 3 and 4 were not near where the torpedo hit, and they rose out of the water, so the boilers in those rooms could not have exploded.

ABBREVIATED VIEWPOINT B

Lusitania (B)

—Warning a ship does not justify sinking it and killing 1200 civilians.

—The munitions of the *Lusitania* would not have exploded when hit by the torpedo.

—The gun cotton was more that 150 feet from where the torpedo struck the ship. There were watertight doors between the two spots. How could the gun cotton have exploded within 1 or 2 seconds of the torpedo hitting 150 feet away?

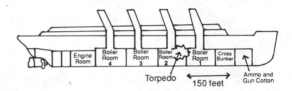

—One diver found a hole on the opposite side of the ship from where the torpedo hit it. The hole was ripped outward, indicating an explosion in that spot. The spot is a boiler room.

—The torpedo hit between the first and second boiler rooms.

—Boilers have frequently exploded when ships have been damaged. The boilers are under tremendous pressure (195 pounds per square inch).

—The *Lusitania* was warned several times by the British navy that there were submarines in the area and to sail in a zigzag route. The *Lusitania's* captain, Captain Turner, sailed straight, making the ship an easy target.

—The *Lusitania* was one of the two fastest ships in the world in 1915. If warships had been sent to "guard" her, she would have had to sail more slowly, making her a better target. Warships had no effective defense against submarines in 1915.

—Many ships had previously been sunk while trying to rescue passengers of torpedoed ships.

Lesson 9: Why Did the United States enter World War I?

Objectives

To find the main idea
To recognize unstated assumptions
To assess cause and effect
To evaluate proof reasoning
To evaluate evidence
To identify various fallacies
To identify words which make value judgments
To identify unclear words

Teaching Ideas

Ask your class why it was difficult for the United States to stay out of World War I. Ask: What was the main cause for United States entry into World War I? Tell them that this question is the focus of this lesson.

Three ways to proceed with the lesson are: (1) have the students evaluate the arguments according to the worksheet, then have them discuss their answers in groups of three and discuss as a class; (2) have students evaluate the viewpoints according to the ARMEAR model explained in the "Guide to Critical Thinking" (p. 18), discuss in groups and discuss as a class; (3) divide the class into pro and con groups on the proposition: submarine warfare by Germany was the main cause for the United States entry into World War I. Along with other research sources, the con group uses Historian A's argument and the pro group uses Historian B's argument. Have the students debate the proposition in small groups (3 against 3) and then, if desired, as a class. Analyze the debate for conclusions, types of reasoning, evidence, and so forth.

To make the lesson less difficult, have students do only Historian A (which contains easier vocabulary) and do only questions 1, 3, and 6 from the worksheet.

You could extend the lesson by having students follow up these two readings with more research and an essay on why the United States entered World War I.

Suggested Analyses
    HISTORIAN A

1. Main point of Historian A

    The main cause for the United States entry into World War I was American loans and trade with the Allies.

2. Unstated assumption (Possible answers)

    —Countries which have more trade with one country than another treat their largest customer better because of the economic trade.

—Diplomatic protests are controlled by economic considerations.

(Note the general phrasing. Ask students if they agree with the assumption. They are likely to conclude that evidence is needed to prove the assumption.)

3. Unstated assumption

It is wrong to make loans to or trade with one side in a war if you cannot make loans to or trade with the other side also.

(Note to students the value judgment in this assumption.)

4. C—The key words are "would have."

5. To answer this question, the students must remember: first, to identify the type of reasoning used; second, to ask the key question; and third, to decide what they think.

a. This sentence is primarily cause-and-effect reasoning based on the cue word "resulted." (It is also sample reasoning.) The author does not make any effort to show the connection between the war trade (the cause) and the prosperity of the United States (the effect). It seems logical that the war trade would help cause prosperity, but there may have been other, more important factors. Without evidence, the author may be guilty of *post hoc* reasoning ("Guide to Critical Thinking," p. 6—the prosperity occurred right after the war began; therefore, the war trade caused the prosperity).

b. This sentence is primarily cause-and-effect reasoning. The cue word here is "made," meaning caused us to be. Again, the connection between the cause (our trade) and the effect (our being unneutral) is unclear. For example, how do we know that the reverse is not true, that our being sympathetic with Britain and France (i.e., unneutral) caused us to trade with these countries? We need to know if there is evidence of the United States being unneutral before the loans were granted. The author may have committed the correlation-as-cause fallacy (p. 6) here.

c. This sentence is a combination of cause-and-effect and proof-by-eliminating-alternatives reasoning. The connection between American loans and supplies to

HISTORIAN A

the Allies (the cause) and German unrestricted submarine warfare (the effect) is not made. Ask your students: what kind of evidence might show the connection between American loans and the German decision to try unrestricted submarine warfare? (Possible answer: Arguments at top level meetings by German leaders that they should try unrestricted submarine warfare to counteract American loans and trade.)

In the proof reasoning the author does not eliminate alternatives to unrestricted submarine warfare. It is hard, however, to think of an effective alternative to submarine warfare that Germany could use to stop American trade.

6. This is strong evidence because the President is showing that what he himself allowed (credits) was not neutral—that is, he has no obvious reason to distort. We might want to see the context of the statement which would give us a better idea of why he said it.

HISTORIAN B

7. Main point of Historian B

    The German submarine campaign was the main reason the United States entered World War I.

8. Unstated assumption (possible answers)

    —People are more precious than property.
    —It is worth going to war over the killing of people.

9. False scenario (p. 6, "Guide to Critical Thinking")

10. False scenario

11. Single causes (p. 6, "Guide to Critical Thinking")

12. Paragraph 1, second sentence—greed; paragraph 4, second to last sentence—indiscriminate destruction

13. Paragraph 3, second sentence—protested; paragraph 5, last sentence—effective; paragraph 7, first sentence—critical

14. Answers will vary on this question.

    a. Historian B shows that propaganda and pro-Allied sympathy would not necessarily have pushed the United States into the war. He does not show, however, that they could not have been the factors that pushed us into war.

b. Historian B argues that the businessmen involved in the war trade had no direct contact with the government and that, therefore, the war trade could not have influenced the government. The *unstated assumption* here—that businessmen need direct contact with government in order to influence it—is highly questionable. For example, Historian A argues that it was the general prosperity of the country which caused American political leaders to be unneutral.

15. This question forces students to look for the part of the argument which is not debating, but rather, which attempts to prove that submarine warfare pushed America into the war. That is, it forces students to examine the part of the argument which supports the main point. Note that in these two short paragraphs there is no evidence to show that submarines were the key factor in the United States entry into the war.

GENERAL QUESTION

16. Answers will vary. Point out that Historian A shows a cause (war trade) for German submarine warfare—the cause argued for by Historian B. Historian B attempts to show that there was no connection between the war trade and the government's decision for war.

UNIT 3
1920s AND THE NEW DEAL

Lesson 10: Identifying and Evaluating Evidence

Objectives

To evaluate evidence
To identify sources

Teaching Ideas

This is a reinforcement lesson on skills from Lessons 1 and 2, so it need not take a lot of time. If students answer the questions for homework, they can compare their answers in small groups and then discuss them as a class fairly quickly.

Suggested Answers

IDENTIFYING EVIDENCE

1. N
2. N
3. S   Amnesty International is the source.
4. N
5. N
6. S   Hiram Evans is the source.
7. S   The *New York Times* is the source.

EVALUATING EVIDENCE

8. Teapot Dome

STRENGTHS

• Allen, as a historian, does not have a reason to lie (R) that we know of.

WEAKNESSES

• It is not a primary (P) source and there is no other (O) evidence supporting his point that Fall made a deal. It is a public (P) source.

SUMMARY

• This source is not as strong as a primary source on the scandal. The author should at least tell the reader what sources he used.

9. New Deal Goals

STRENGTHS

• It is a primary (P) source.

WEAKNESSES

• Roosevelt has a reason to lie (R) about some things since it is a public (P) statement. He is certainly not going to explain points that will hurt some groups. He can be more blunt than before the election, but he cannot say things that will erode his political support. On the other hand, the speech should be a clear statement of the broad goals of the program. There is no other (O) evidence of his goals, which could shed light on what goals were most important.

SUMMARY
- Overall this is a good source to use to get an idea of Roosevelt's goals in 1933, however, more sources are needed.

10. Republic Steel Plant Violence—*Times* Article

STRENGTHS
- It was written soon after the event.

WEAKNESSES
- Since the article quotes the police, it is fairly clear that the newspaper did not have a reporter on the scene. Thus, it was not a primary (P) source. Moreover, the police have a strong reason to lie (R) to protect themselves. There is no other (O) evidence to support the claims made, and the article, as well as the police statement, is public (P)—meant to influence people.

SUMMARY
- This is a very weak source.

11. Republic Steel Plant Violence—Senate report on the Paramount film

STRENGTHS
- The film is a primary (P) source, and the film just took in what happened so it had no obvious reason to lie (R).

WEAKNESSES
- There is no other (O) evidence supporting the viewpoint that the police started the riot. The question of why the confrontation was filmed raises the possibility that it was to influence opinion afterward (P—public source) by representing the strikers' point of view. Thus, the filmmakers may have had a reason to lie (R).

SUMMARY
- Overall, this is a much stronger source than the *Times* article (#10), but the film could have distorted what happened, for example, by focusing the camera on the police when the strikers were throwing things or shooting.

Lesson 11: Identifying and Evaluating Comparisons

Objectives

To identify and evaluate comparisons

Teaching Ideas

The section on identifying comparisons should not be too difficult and can be done quickly. Cue students to watch for comparative words. The section on evaluating comparisons should be more challenging and may lead to some problematic responses. Try to focus on the process of evaluating comparisons rather than on right answers. Items 9 and 11 involve the selection of statistics for specific years which suggests the possibility of the fallacy of special pleading (p. 11, "Guide to Critical Thinking").

Suggested Answers

IDENTIFYING COMPARISONS

1. C "Better" indicates a comparison.
2. N
3. N
4. C
5. N
6. C "More" indicates a comparison.
7. C "Better" indicates a comparison.
8. N

EVALUATING COMPARISONS

9. There are a number of possible differences which make us question the comparison. Inflation or increased advertising rates could account for some of the increase in the amount spent on advertising. Or a new mode for advertising, such as radio, may have made advertising more effective, leading to more use of it.

10. It is likely that farmers' income went down while their expenses went up. We would need to know more, however, about the amount of crops sold. If the amount sold increased dramatically, then farm income may have gone up despite lower prices. They are the same people performing the same job, so the comparison seems reasonable.

11. It looks like the unemployment rate dropped, but we would rather see percentages (a better comparative indicator) than absolute numbers. (Percentages are given in item #12, and actually show a more dramatic improvement.) The other question, as in item 9, is why these years were selected. If 1934 and 1938 were used, a different picture would emerge. So this

is an example of special pleading. It is not clear that item 9 commits this fallacy, but it is clear that this argument does.

12. As mentioned above, if 1934 and 1938 are selected, the argument could be made that the New Deal made very little difference in the economy.

Lesson 12: Analyzing Cause and Effect

Objectives

To identify and evaluate cause-and-effect reasoning

Teaching Ideas

Have students read the introduction and, if necessary, ask questions to make sure they understand it. Have them read the three viewpoints and explain which viewpoint is strongest under question 1. Then have them discuss their answers in small groups and as a class. If you did Lesson 4 with this class, you can refer back to it to guide students.

The section on identifying cause-and-effect arguments is meant to be a quick follow-up lesson. Have students answer the questions in this section and discuss as a class.

Suggested Answers

CONNECTION

1. Strongest viewpoint

   Based on the criterion of connecting Prohibition (the proposed cause) to the expansion of organized crime (the effect), the best answer is A. This viewpoint connects the illegality of alcohol to smaller supply. Smaller supply connects to higher prices and profits, with organized crime filling the demand and raking in easy money.

   Historian B says that many people refused to obey the Volstead Act but does not explain how this opposition led to more organized crime. Historian C describes the many methods used by organized crime to distribute and sell alcohol, but does not show how Prohibition led to more organized crime. The last sentences in both Historian B and C are irrelevant to the causes for organized crime.

IDENTIFYING CAUSE-AND-EFFECT ARGUMENTS

2. N   No cause for why he drives or walks is proposed.

3. C   cause—$600 to fix car
       effect—cancelled the trip

4. C   cause—new industrialization
       effect—leisure time to masses

5. C   causes—wave of strikes and Communist Party
       effect—anti-radicalism reaction in the United States

6. N   No cause for why he did not fear ridicule is proposed.

7. N   No cause is proposed for why the flapper wanted the same social freedom as men.

Lesson 13: Were Sacco and Vanzetti Guilty?

Objectives

To evaluate evidence

Teaching Ideas

Some students may get frustrated by the contradictory nature of the information in this lesson. They may want a clear, simple answer, especially at the end of the lesson. Don't give it to them.

Begin by asking students if making a historical judgment about whether someone committed a crime is the same as making a legal judgment in court that someone is guilty of committing a crime. (No. We might feel someone should be found not guilty in court but feel he or she probably committed the crime. In court we have to prove beyond a reasonable doubt, while in history we judge whether something happened if there is more evidence to show it happened than to show it did not happen.) Tell your students that today's class will deal with the historical question of whether Sacco and Vanzetti committed the murder and the legal question of whether they should have been found guilty in court.

For homework, have the students sort the information into evidence that could be used to show guilt (G), to show innocence (I), or that cannot be used to show guilt or innocence (N), then write their argument in favor of or against Sacco and Vanzetti. Group students by their preferences and have them debate the issue as a class.

After the debate, discuss the issue of whether Sacco and Vanzetti should have been found guilty in court. Make sure students realize this is a separate question. Ask students which information would not be available to the jury. Have them decide, as best they can, based only on the information available to the jury.

Have students consider the photograph of Sacco and Vanzetti and discuss their answers.

Obviously there is a great deal more information that could be researched on this controversial case. If students get interested and want to do more research, wonderful!

Suggested Answers

1. N
2. G   It is not very strong, but it could be used by prosecutors.

3. N It can be used by prosecutors (G) if combined with number 4.

4. G Now information 3 is significant.

5. G

6. G

7. G Anarchism should be interesting to discuss. Do students think that radicals are more likely to commit violent crimes? You could discuss the political climate of the 1920s at this point. Some students should question why pacifists were carrying guns.

8. I It shows that Sacco and Vanzetti's behavior in 5 and 6 might be due to the circumstances, not to their guilt.

9. I Same as information 8

10. G

11. N It shows that perhaps the police were unfair, but it does not show that Sacco and Vanzetti were innocent.

12. N

13. I

14. I or G Some witnesses identified Sacco, but the reliability of witnesses' testimony is weakened.

15. N See information 11, above.

16. G or I It depends on which part is emphasized.

17. I

18. I

19. I It shows a lack of reliability among witnesses.

20. I

21. G

22. G

23. I

24. I

25. G This weakens the defense's case.

26. I

27. G It weakens Madeiros's confession.

28. G

29. G

30. I

31. I

32. I The implication is that someone (the police or

prosecution, perhaps) fired a fourth bullet through Sacco's gun and then added the shell to the evidence to get Sacco convicted. This is an inference—it isn't proven.

33. I   This weakens the cap as evidence (#28).

34. I

35. I

36. I

37. I   If Sacco committed the crime, why would he let them test his gun?

38. I

39. I

ARGUING THE CASE   Answers are based on student assessment of the information.

PHOTOGRAPH   The prosecution might emphasize the foreign appearance of the men, Vanzetti especially. The defense would emphasize the upstanding appearance of the two men—their ties, neat shirts, etc.

Lesson 14: What Caused the Great Depression?

Objectives

To identify and evaluate evidence
To find the main idea
To recognize unstated assumptions
To assess cause and effect
To relate relevant information to hypotheses

Teaching Ideas

Have students read through the introductory section containing the glossary of terms. Question students to make sure they understand these terms. You may also want to supplement the terms with a discussion of how money is created by banks using the fractional reserve system. Most economics books have a few pages on the creation of money. Understanding how money is created is important to understanding Historian E's argument.

Next, have students read the relevant information and Historians A and B and answer the questions. Discuss their answers, then move on through the other historians and questions.

You can make the lesson less difficult by skipping Historian F (and possibly Historian E) and questions 4, 9, 10, and 11.

Some students may conclude that none of the viewpoints is very good. In this instance, that may not be such a bad conclusion. Economist Peter Temin has argued that none of the hypotheses (interpretations) of the causes of the Great Depression has been adequately tested.

Suggested Answers
HISTORIANS A AND B

1. Main point of Historian A: The weaknesses of the American economy (declining industries, technological unemployment, unequal distribution of income, and foreign trade problems) were the main cause of the Depression.

2. Main point of Historian B: The main cause of the Great Depression was the unequal distribution of income in the 1920s.

3. Based on the key question for cause-and-effect reasoning (Does the historian show the connection between the cause and the effect?), Historian B has the stronger explanation. Historian B at least explains that unequal distribution of income leads to overpro-

duction, but does not explain how overproduction leads to depression. Historian A does not explain how *any* of his causes led to the Depression.

4. Possible assumptions

—The stock crash was equal to the Depression.

—Once the stock market crashed the Depression was inevitable.

—When the stock market crashed America was immediately plunged into the Depression.

—The stock market crash was the only cause of the Depression.

5. Weaknesses

a. Historian A—Relevant information 5 weakens this viewpoint. It also has all the weaknesses listed below for Historian B.

b. Historian B—Relevant information 3 shows that the increase in production and the decrease in consumption, due to unequal distribution of income, could not have been important. Even if the rich people used all of their money for production and the poor used all of theirs for consumption, the change in income would only account for a 2% decrease in consumption—not a significant factor in the 36% decrease in national income from 1929 to 1933.

Relevant information 4 also hurts this argument since it shows that the assumption that crashes lead inevitably to depressions is not warranted.

Both Historians A and B commit the *post hoc* fallacy (p. 6, "Guide to Critical Thinking"). They reason that since the Depression followed the stock crash, the stock crash must have caused the Depression.

HISTORIANS C AND D

6. Historian C gives a clearly stronger argument, by explaining how the stock crash would cause a decline in spending and investment, thus reducing GNP. Historian D only shows what caused the bull market and why the market fell once the prices started to decline.

7. Historian C—Relevant information 1 and 2 show that the stock market crash was not significant compared to the decline in national income which followed it. It may be, as one economist put it, that the stock

crash was the initial shock which led to a macro-economic meltdown. Even if this is true, there needs to be more explanation on how the stock market crash caused the meltdown.

Relevant information 4 weakens the argument, as explained for Historian B. The first paragraph of Historian E also weakens this argument since he points out that everyone agrees that there was a recession in 1929. So the stock crash may have caused a recession in 1929. The question is why the economy did not recover in 1930.

HISTORIAN E

8. Main point of Historian E: The decline in the money supply, due to the bank panic and the restrictive policies of the Federal Reserve Bank, was the primary cause of the Great Depression.

9. A weakness in Historian E's argument could be correlation as cause. How do we know that the decline in national income did not cause the decline in the money supply, rather than the other way around? See the answer for question 10, Historian F for an explanation of the debate between Historians E and F on this point.

HISTORIAN F

10. Main point of Historian F: The decline in spending in 1930 was the main cause of the Great Depression.

11. Several possible answers: What factors does he think caused spending to decline so much in 1930? How low were interest rates? Were all interest rates low?

12. Historian F—Relevant information 6 might weaken his case, but we do not know. The argument is quite complex between these two historians. Historian E claims that the other interest rates are a better indicator of the supply and demand for money, while Historian F claims that short-term interest rates are the key indicator.

GENERAL QUESTIONS

13. Solutions for depressions: Answers will vary. Some reasonable inferences are:

Historian B—Equalize wealth more. (Some New Deal programs and tax legislation tried to do this.)

Historian D—Regulate the stock market to control speculation and buying on margin. (The Securities and Exchange Commission was set up to do this.)

Historian E—Try a more expansionary monetary

policy during a depression. Start insuring bank deposits to prevent bank panics (such as the FDIC).

Historian F—Stimulate more spending during a depression. (This would be done through the Keynesian policy of deficit spending.)

14. Student answers will vary depending on their assessments of the viewpoints. Historians E and F should get most of the votes the way the lesson is written.

Lesson 15: What Should Be Done to Cure the Depression

Objectives

To assess cause and effect
To recognize unstated assumptions

Teaching Ideas

It is best to use this lesson *before* students have read anything about the New Deal, but after they have studied the causes of the Depression.

Have students fill in the worksheet for homework and have them discuss their answers in small groups, trying to convince one another that their selections would work best. Then discuss the choices as a class. Which would they do? Which proposals are not good choices? Why? Are there other ideas, not in the lesson, they think should have been tried?

Another aspect you could focus on is the political spectrum. Use the sheet explaining the political spectrum (p. 83), if necessary, and then have students label each proposal A–E, as directed on p. 84.

After students complete the lesson, have them try to find examples of at least four of the proposals that were actually tried in the United States or in other countries in the 1920s and 1930s. The suggested answer section on the political spectrum indicates where some of the proposals were really tried.

Suggested Answers

TOP AND BOTTOM
RANKED CHOICES

The ranking is a matter of opinion by the students, but make them defend their choices with good reasons. Watch for cause-and-effect reasoning and unstated assumptions.

WHERE THE PROPOSALS
MIGHT BE ON THE
POLITICAL SPECTRUM

(There can be reasonable differences of opinion about the answers. Ask students to support their choices.)

1. A or B Proposed by Rexford Tugwell, one of FDR's "brain trust"

2. D

3. D This is similar to the actual set up of the NRA (National Recovery Administration). It is important to note from this that originally the New Deal was conservative (pro-business), at least to some extent.

4. D Similar to President Hoover's position

5. B

6. B Similar to the Keynesian position

7. A Huey Long's position

8. E The Fascist solution to the Depression—this is what Germany tried under the Nazis. Interestingly enough, "A" would be an acceptable answer also.

9. A The Communist solution

10. D Similar to President Hoover's position

Lesson 16: Was the New Deal Good or Bad for the Country?

Objectives

To find the main idea
To identify evidence
To recognize unstated assumptions
To assess cause and effect
To evaluate generalizations
To identify the false scenario fallacy

Teaching Ideas

Have the students read the two viewpoints and answer the questions, then discuss their answers as a class. Or you could ask students which viewpoint they feel is stronger (Question 9) and just discuss that question, focusing on the strengths and weaknesses of the two arguments. Or you could have students evaluate the arguments according to the ARMEAR Model (p. 18, "Guide to Critical Thinking").

Both of these arguments are weak due primarily to their brevity and lack of evidence. An interesting assignment would be to have students choose one of the arguments and write an improved version of it (perhaps with specific suggestions, such as including two pieces of evidence).

Use the viewpoints as a springboard for further research and position papers on the New Deal.

Suggested Answers
HISTORIAN A

1. Possible main points

   —The New Deal was bad for our country.

   —The New Deal was a failure.

2. None. No sources are given.

3. Possible assumptions

   —The economy functions normally (and well) when intellectuals or socialists are not involved in it.

   —Intellectuals and socialists hurt the economy.

4. Evaluate

   Cause and effect—How do we know the New Deal caused the debt increase? Maybe something else caused it, such as the Depression.

   Generalization—Why were these particular years selected to compare? Could this be the fallacy of special pleading?

Assumption—Is this increase in debt really bad?

HISTORIAN B

5. Possible main points

—The New Deal helped our country.

—The New Deal reformed and saved our capitalist system.

6. None. No sources are included.

7. Fallacy

False scenario (p. 6, "Guide to Critical Thinking")

8. This is a generalization. We want to know if the author's sample is representative of the American public as a whole. Most likely the author did not take a poll at all, so the sample is really more of a hunch. Also, this is a hard generalization—if only one person starved, this exaggerated claim is disproved.

CARTOONS

9. This is a matter of opinion, but must be based on sound reasons.

Cartoon A, "Old Reliable," is critical of the New Deal, so it would support Historian A.

Cartoon B, "Yes, You Remembered Me," is favorable to the New Deal, so it would support Historian B.

UNIT 4
FOREIGN POLICY SINCE 1945

Lesson 17: Assessing the Reliability of Sources

Objectives

To evaluate evidence

Teaching Ideas

This is a reinforcement lesson on evaluating evidence (see Lessons 2 and 10). Students should fill in the strengths and weaknesses, then you can discuss them as a class. The discussion should go fairly quickly, but there are likely to be some disagreements and gray areas. Focus on the process, not right answers.

Some students may get confused if they do not know much about the topics discussed in each problem (the Cold War, fall of China, and so forth).

Suggested Answers

1. Cold War—Byrnes' book

STRENGTHS
• Byrnes is a primary source (P).

WEAKNESSES
• Byrnes has a reason to lie (R) when blaming the Cold War on the Soviets rather than his own government; there is no other (O) evidence offered here to support his views; and it is a public (P) statement.

SUMMARY
• We would need more evidence of Soviet violations to corroborate Byrnes' evidence.

2. Fall of China—Acheson's article

STRENGTHS
• Acheson is a primary (P) source on United States policy toward China, but not about events in China. On the other hand, he would have access to a lot of information on events in China.

WEAKNESSES
• Acheson has a reason to lie (R) to protect himself and the State Department; there is no other (O) evidence to support his claims; and it is a public (P) statement.

SUMMARY
• This is weak evidence, due to Acheson's reason to lie.

3. North Korean Attack—UN statements

STRENGTHS
• There is a great deal of evidence other (O) than the UN statements.

WEAKNESSES
• None of the evidence is from primary (P) sources,

unless the newspapers had reporters on the scene at the time of the attack. The UN statements are certainly secondary sources regarding the attack. As far as we know, all the countries had a reason to lie (R) as this is an issue dividing Communist from non-Communist countries. The UN statements are public (P).

SUMMARY
- The corroboration makes it strong evidence.

4. Missiles in Cuba—aerial photographs

STRENGTHS
- The photographs are primary sources (P) and have no reason to lie (R), although they could have been staged or doctored. There is other (O) evidence supporting the point that the Soviets had missiles there; and, inasmuch as the Soviets did not know that they were being photographed, the photos are private (P). The photos were used publicly by the United States.

WEAKNESSES
- None

SUMMARY
- This is very strong evidence.

5. Marshall Plan—statement by Marshall

STRENGTHS
- Marshall is a primary source (P).

WEAKNESSES
- Marshall is making a public statement (P), so he has a reason to lie (R), and there is no other evidence supporting his points.

SUMMARY
- Despite its weaknesses, this is an important piece of evidence in determining why the United States started the Marshall Plan. We just need other evidence to verify it.

Lesson 18: Identifying Assumptions and Analyzing Value Judgments

Objectives

To identify unstated assumptions
To analyze value judgments

Teaching Ideas

Have students complete the section on identifying unstated assumptions, compare answers in small groups, and discuss their answers as a class. Students may have to refer several times to the section on **Assumptions** in the "Guide to Critical Thinking" (p. 15).

Go over the first item in the section on value judgments (Question #7) to make sure students understand what they are doing. Then have them individually do items 8, 9, and 10, compare their analyses in small groups, and discuss as a class. After you finish this method of analyzing value judgments, you might want to refer students to the other tests for value judgments (p. 17, "Guide to Critical Thinking"):

—What would society be like if everyone believed and acted on this value?

—Would you want the value applied to you?

Have students apply these questions to the value judgments in questions 7–10. For example, in number 7 the value judgment is: You should always keep a promise. We could test the worthiness of this claim by asking the two questions. (Society would be better off if all people kept their promises. Most people would want other people to keep their promises.)

EXTENDING THE LESSON

A very interesting way to extend the lesson is to do the following exercise which reveals students' assumptions.

Give every student a handout with a statement on it about a battle. Instruct them to add at least two more sentences to the story, including the situation leading up to the battle. Half the class will get the statement, "American forces attacked Soviet troops in Germany." The other half get the statement, "Soviet forces attacked American troops in Germany." It is important that students not know that they have different statements. After they have added to the statements, you can ask for volunteers to read theirs and ask if anyone recognizes assumptions in the completions. Or you could ask how many students thought the attackers were to blame. If more hands go up from the students who have the statement with the Soviets attacking, you can ask why. What are many people assuming about Soviet and American motives?

Suggested Answers

IDENTIFY UNSTATED
ASSUMPTIONS

1. —I make better decisions.

   —I have more power than you (overrule).

   —You do not make very good decisions—you need guidance.

2. —When a teacher wants to see you after school, you have done something wrong (or you are in trouble).

3. —The Soviets do not respect compromise.

   —The Soviets will take whatever they can get.

   —The Soviets will not compromise if we compromise.

4. —Communism spreads to areas where there are economic troubles.

   —People are attracted to Communism for economic reasons.

5. —United States troops would have made the difference in the Civil War—they would have brought about victory.

   —Nationalist victory in China was more important to the United States than having men killed in a war.

   —What happened in China (or stopping Communism) is important to the United States.

6. —The threat of nuclear retaliation will be effective in stopping aggression.

VALUE JUDGMENTS

7. Done for them

8. Free elections

   Conclusion: The U.S.S.R. caused the problems in eastern Europe.

   Factual: The U.S.S.R. promised free elections but did not hold them.

   Value: Countries should keep their promises.

   Case: Suppose a country promised to hold free elections but then found that its most feared enemies would be elected.

   (Another value judgment is: Free elections are important. This claim can be explored also.)

9. Lend-lease

   Conclusion: Cutting off lend-lease was justified.

   Factual: The U.S.S.R. did not appreciate our aid.

   Value: Countries are justified in cutting aid to countries which do not appreciate it.

   Case: Suppose a country was giving aid to people starving due to a famine. Would it be justified in cutting the aid if the government of the famine-stricken country did not appreciate it?

10. German attack

    Conclusion: The Russians were justified in taking over eastern Europe.

    Factual: The U.S.S.R. took eastern Europe to prevent future attack.

    Value: Countries are justified in taking over other countries in order to prevent possible future attack.

    Case: Would the largest country in the world be justified in taking over ten other countries to prevent a possible future attack by a very small country?

Lesson 19: Identifying and Analyzing Types of Reasoning

Objectives

To identify and evaluate cause and effect
To identify and evaluate generalizations
To identify and evaluate comparisons
To identify the golden mean and big fig fallacies

Teaching Ideas

Have the students fill in the answers individually and share their answers in small groups, where they can help one another. Discuss their answers as a class. Since there are several types of reasoning possible for some items, listen for student reasons—the answers below are suggestive, not all inclusive. The fallacy in number 8 is not explained anywhere in this book, so students will have to consider it carefully rather than naming it.

Suggested Answers

TYPES OF REASONING

1. Football Game

TYPE

• Cause and effect

EVALUATION

• The connection of the "bad call" to the outcome is not clear. It is extremely unlikely that one play alone determined the outcome of a whole game. Besides, it sounds like the other team won by a wide margin ("rolled over us"). There are a number of other possible causes, such as the other team was better. This is a weak argument.

2. Contras

TYPE

• Mainly comparison but also cause and effect

EVALUATION

• Listen to arguments on whether the similarities (its domination by a big power in both cases) outweigh the differences (our army did not march in with the rebels, we are not imposing a totalitarian regime, etc.).

3. Poll on North

TYPE

• Generalization

EVALUATION

• Most polls today are randomly selected. The sample is very small but the samples usually represent the public well. The polling company claims it is accurate within 4%.

4. Missiles in Cuba

TYPE

• Comparison

EVALUATION • Listen for reasons on both sides. In terms of a nuclear attack there may be no significant difference. In terms of political results from Soviet missiles in Cuba, however, the effects may be significant.

5. Kennedy and *The Guns of August*

TYPE • Comparison; also cause and effect

EVALUATION • The situation in 1962 may have been very different from that in 1914. Students should consider alliances, politics at home, technology, communication, geography, military balances, and so forth.

6. Korea

TYPE • Cause and effect

EVALUATION • The drive through North Korea probably led to the Chinese invasion, but we would like to see some evidence to show the connection. Maybe the Chinese would have invaded anyway. The argument would have been much stronger if the author included warnings by the Chinese that they would invade if the UN army drove further north.

EVALUATE 7. Cuban Missile Crisis

This is the golden mean fallacy (p. 13, "Guide to Critical Thinking").

8. Nicaraguan threat to Central America

This is the fallacy of the "Big Fig" (Big Figure). Compare the Honduras soldier to the Nicaragua soldier. The Nicaraguan army is roughly three times as large as the Honduran army, but the figure for Nicaragua is three times as high *and* three times as wide or roughly nine times as large to the eye. The visual effect is to exaggerate the Nicaraguan threat.

Lesson 20: Was the United States Justified in Dropping the Atomic Bombs on Japan?

Objectives

To find the main idea
To recognize unstated assumptions
To evaluate evidence
To evaluate generalizations
To evaluate comparisons
To evaluate cause and effect
To relate hypotheses to relevant information
To analyze value judgments
To evaluate proof by evidence and proof by eliminating
    alternatives

Teaching Ideas

It is recommended that you begin the lesson with the introductory section followed by the Atomic Bomb—Values Survey (p. 104, Student Text). This will get some of the value issues out in the open. The discussion of the survey tends to be lively. You can help students examine their value positions by asking questions about the underlying beliefs, as explained on p. 17 of the "Guide to Critical Thinking." Does warning always make an action justifiable? (Item 1) Does saving more lives in the end always make an action justifiable? (Item 2) Is continuing military action when the other side is trying to surrender always wrong? (Item 4) And so on. You can conclude this part of the lesson by asking if people who examine the same information but who have different values will arrive at the same conclusions. (No. For example, if you believe warning the enemy does not justify the bombings, then finding information about warning the Japanese will not mean very much and probably will not be emphasized in your interpretation. Beliefs shape the use of evidence.)

Tell the students that you are going to examine whether some of the claims made in the values survey actually took place. (Did we warn the Japanese? Were they really trying to surrender?) There are a number of options for using the two viewpoints. First, you could divide the class by their preferences into pro and con to debate in small groups the proposition that the United States was justified in dropping the atomic bombs. (Use the students who are undecided to even off the two groups.) Before the students debate, give them 5 or 10 minutes to organize by writing five arguments for their side. Cue them to focus on the weak points of the other viewpoint, especially evidence, reasoning, and assumptions.

A second method is to have students evaluate the two viewpoints according to the ARMEAR model (p. 18, "Guide to Critical Thinking"). Or you could have the class read and evaluate Historian A, discuss it, and then read Historian B, evaluate and discuss it. Remind students that there is relevant information that should be used, along with any other information they can think of, in their evaluations. The suggested answers are done according to the ARMEAR model.

You could get away from a step-by-step model by just telling the students to evaluate the two viewpoints and decide which is stronger. You could get away from a class analysis by having small groups decide which viewpoint is stronger and explain why in a report to the class.

Some students may become frustrated by the lack of resolution of many of the questions raised in this topic. Each argument may have a strong counterargument. They may push you for your analysis, that is, to resolve the issues for them. Resist the temptation.

A good concluding activity is to have students write their own interpretation of whether the United States was justified in dropping the bombs (Historian C?). You could, for example, require them to include two or three pieces of evidence and to argue that this evidence should be believed.

Suggested Answers
ARMEAR MODEL

ANALYSIS OF HISTORIAN A

(Some ideas for discussion—this is a partial analysis.)

A (Author)—Students might conclude that the author is Japanese or at least not American. He is, however, actually American.

R (Relevant Information)—Relevant information number 1 is related to paragraph 6, endnote 6. It should make us question the reliability of Historian A, since it seems to show that Historian A took a quote by President Truman out of context to prove something which Truman never intended.

Relevant information 3 and 5 lend support to Historian A's interpretation.

M (Main Point)—The United States was not justified in dropping the atomic bombs on Japan.

E (Evidence)—The evidence by Stimson (endnotes 2, 5, 7) and Byrnes (endnotes 1, 7) is strong because they

HISTORIAN A

have no reason to distort what they say—it makes them look bad.

The evidence by Szilard (endnote 2) is weaker. Szilard was opposed to the use of the bomb, which makes him a biased recorder of what Byrnes said.

The evidence of Eisenhower and Leahy (endnote 8) is weak because these men have a reason to distort (they do not want to be identified with the use of atomic weapons). Also, they, along with LeMay, might not want to give credit for the Japanese defeat to the atomic bombs rather than to the efforts of their own forces (army, navy, and air force, respectively).

A (Assumptions)—Paragraph 2: A policy (such as unconditional surrender) which is changed later is not a worthy enough policy for which to kill people. This is an interesting proposition to discuss. Could the policy have been worthy enough at one point, but not at a later point? Note that relevant information 5 is related to this question.

R (Reasoning)

- Generalization (Paragraph 10)—The sample of military leaders from paragraph 10, endnote 8 is impressive in that they are leaders from that time. It is only three leaders, however. What about the others? One could reasonably question whether the military was divided about whether to use the bomb. If there were military leaders in favor of using the bomb, this historian might be guilty of special pleading (p. 11, "Guide to Critical Thinking").

- Proof by Evidence (throughout)—The evidence presented brings up some interesting points. Some of the key pieces of evidence are presented by Secretary of War Stimson and Secretary of State Byrnes. If we assume for a moment that the evidence conclusively shows that Stimson and Byrnes were interested in the atomic bomb for diplomatic reasons, does this show that the bomb was dropped for diplomatic reasons? Not necessarily. There were many other advisers involved and President Truman seems to have been the final decision-maker (the buck stopped there). We need to know more about how important Stimson and Byrnes were to the actual decision, about the decision-making process, and about Truman's motives for dropping the bomb.

Other evidence seems to indicate that President Truman was tougher with the Russians after the bomb was successfully tested. This does not mean, however, that the primary motivation for dropping the bomb was diplomatic advantage over the Russians. Diplomatic advantage could have been an incidental benefit to be gained from a decision made for other, more important reasons (perhaps saving lives.)

- Cause and Effect—The evidence showing that American leaders wanted to stop Soviet expansion in Asia only provides a possible motive for dropping the atomic bombs on Japan. It does not show that the bombs were used primarily for diplomatic reasons. In fact, it does not really show that the bombs were used to stop Russian expansion at all—it only hints at it. There could be other, more important, causes for dropping the bombs.

ARMEAR MODEL

ANALYSIS OF HISTORIAN B

(Some ideas for discussion—this is a partial analysis.)

A (Author)—This author seems pro-American and is an American.

R (Relevant Information)—Relevant Information 2 lends some support to Historian B's argument in paragraph 8.

M (Main Point)—The United States was justified in dropping the atomic bombs on Japan.

E (Evidence)—The evidence in endnotes 2, 3, and 5 is from secondary sources. They will need to be checked for accuracy against primary evidence.

The evidence in endnote 8 is strong, since the United States leaders would have no reason to demand surrender unless they meant it. It is possible, however, that the American government was making different demands privately. (There is no evidence of this.)

The evidence in endnote 9 is weakened by the fact that it is a public statement and Suzuki might have a reason to distort. That is, the Japanese government might have felt that to keep morale up it had to say it would ignore demands for surrender.

A (Assumptions)—Paragraph 4: A policy which hurts a war effort should not be adopted. You might want to ask: Is protesting against a war which you feel is

HISTORIAN B

misguided wrong? Is it always wrong for a government official to question a policy during a war which he/she feels is wrong, even if it hurts the war effort? Just what helps or hurts war efforts?

R (Reasoning)

- Proof by Evidence (throughout)—The key question for proof by evidence is: Does the evidence prove the point? The evidence presented in paragraphs 3, 4, and 5 does make the reader question whether Japan was close to anything like unconditional surrender. Questions could still be raised on this point however. Was unconditional surrender really worth insisting on to the point of using atomic weapons? Does the information that the Japanese leaders were deadlocked really have any bearing on our decision to drop the bombs? After all, we did not know what they were saying in their meetings. We dropped the bombs without pursuing any negotiations with the Japanese. Is what they were thinking really relevant if we did not even talk with them?

  The evidence of the Interim Committee (paragraph 8) puts the opposition of some scientists to dropping the bomb into perspective by showing that other scientists were in favor of a military use of the bomb. It does not prove, however, that the bomb was not dropped for diplomatic reasons. Maybe the members of the Committee were thinking of the diplomatic advantages of the bomb when they decided that it was too risky to demonstrate the bomb to Japanese leaders.

  The evidence that we warned the Japanese (paragraph 9) is tricky. Students should note that in endnote 8 there is no mention of the words "atomic bomb" or "bomb." Did this message really warn the Japanese of what was to come?

- Proof by Eliminating Alternatives—The key question for proof by eliminating alternatives is: Are all the alternatives really eliminated? The eliminating-alternatives reasoning used in paragraph 6 might be restated: President Truman *could not* have rushed the dropping of the bombs to stop Russian entry into the war, since he did not control the dates of the bombings. This argument does make the reader think that stopping the Russians may not have been the highest priority. On the other hand, Truman may have made it clear that the bombs should be dropped as soon as possible, but left the exact days of the bombings to the military. The question at the end of paragraph 6 could be answered: Truman could get both unconditional surrender and the end of the war before Russia entered it by using the bombs.

The eliminating-alternatives reasoning in paragraph 7 is weak. The fact that we did not actually scare the Russians with the atomic bomb has no bearing on whether we intended to scare them with the bomb.

- Comparison—The key question for the comparison reasoning in paragraph 2 is: Are the two cases similar enough to make the conclusion a good one? The argument might be restated: Unconditional surrender would have made for a better peace at the end of World War I; therefore, it was needed at the end of World War II. The discussion of the similarities and differences between these two cases could be quite interesting.

GENERAL COMMENTS

Both historians engage in hypothetical reasoning, for example: "If the United States had not dropped the bombs, the Japanese would have surrendered soon anyway." In one sense this reasoning commits the fallacy of false scenario (p. 6, "Guide to Critical Thinking"). The issue of whether the United States was justified in dropping the atomic bombs, however, seems inextricably entwined with hypothetical reasoning. Thus, the evaluation of interpretations on the issue should include analysis of hypothetical reasoning based on the evidence presented that such-and-such would have happened if something else had happened. In short, how reasonably are the hypothetical results argued?

You might want to discuss with your students the whole philosophical question of hypothetical scenarios in history. Some historians have argued that econometric works, such as Robert Fogel's *Railroads and American Economic Growth*, are not real history, since they remove some element (railroads in this case) from history and then project what might have occurred without that element. Other historians argue that a great deal of history involves hypothetical reasoning by implication. Merely stating that something (like railroads) was a key factor in events (like economic growth) is by implication making a hypothetical argument. That is, it is arguing that, without that one element, present events would have been significantly different. It is an interesting question to discuss.

The issue of motivation (a type of cause) is a key factor in the analysis of the dropping of the atomic bombs. It is partly the elusiveness of pinning down the motivation of historical figures that has led to such different interpretations of this topic. You might want to discuss the question of motivation with your students.

Lesson 21: Who Primarily Caused the Cold War?

Objectives

To find the main idea
To recognize value claims and unstated assumptions
To evaluate evidence
To evaluate comparisons
To evaluate cause and effect
To identify fallacies—*ad hominem*, *post hoc*, false
      scenario, special pleading

Teaching Ideas

Start the lesson by having students read the overview of the Cold War and asking them questions to make sure they understand it.

As in Lesson 20, there are a number of ways to conduct the lesson. You could have small group debates on the question: Who was primarily responsible for starting the Cold War? Or you could have one large debate. Second, you could evaluate the viewpoints according to the ARMEAR model. Remind students that relevant information is included in the lesson (p. 115, Student Text). Third, you could have students make group reports on which viewpoint is stronger and why. All of these strategies are described in more detail in the teaching ideas section of the Teacher's Guide for Lesson 20 (p. 104).

Another option for this lesson is to have students read the two viewpoints and write the strengths and weaknesses of each. Then discuss these in small groups and as a class. The suggested answers section below gives some interesting points to raise for a discussion of strengths and weaknesses.

You could conclude the lesson by having students write an evaluation of one of the viewpoints or by having them write their own interpretation of the origins of the Cold War, either with or without outside research.

Suggested Answers
INTERPRETATION A

1. Paragraph 1—"Naively patriotic" is an *ad hominem* fallacy (p. 14, "Guide to Critical Thinking").

2. Paragraph 2—This paragraph makes the argument that a country is justified in taking an area as a sphere of influence in order to deter a possible future invasion. Is this justified? In all cases? See Lesson 18 for an example of evaluating value positions.

INTERPRETATION A

3. Paragraph 3—Comparison of the two spheres—Are they really similar? Interpretation B will argue that they are not.

4. Paragraph 4—The quote by Churchill (endnote 1) is strong evidence that an agreement was made. Did Churchill mean, however, that this agreement would set up spheres of influence after World War II?

5. Paragraph 6—Endnote 4 does not really support the contention that Bulgaria's elections were the freest in the country's history. The evidence says that there was the widest participation. We have to be skeptical since the evidence for "widest participation" comes from Molotov, who has a reason to distort and is not a primary source. The *New York Times* part of the evidence only says the elections were orderly. Elections in which soldiers force people to vote, and to vote a particular way, would both be orderly and have a high participation rate, but would not be free.

6. Paragraph 7—Endnote 5 is all by secondary sources. How did these historians learn that the Communists were popular and the elections were free?

7. Paragraph 8—Endnote 8 is strong in that Roosevelt has no reason to distort. We need to know more, however, about the context of Roosevelt's remarks. Also, what does he mean by the word "basis"?

8. Paragraph 9—Roosevelt's remarks may have prompted Stalin to think that American concern for eastern Europe was due to domestic politics in the United States. Roosevelt may not have believed what he said to Stalin. Roosevelt may have used the American voters of eastern European descent as an argument to get Stalin to agree to free elections. The President's main goal may really have been to secure free elections.

9. Paragraph 10—The summarizing statement that the three countries had reached "a series of agreements and understandings about the Soviet sphere of influence in eastern Europe" is not warranted from the previous arguments. Britain and Russia had an agreement about some countries in eastern Europe, and all three had an agreement on Poland. But the agreement on Poland declared the intent to carry out free elections and the Soviets did not do that. Several countries taken by the Soviets (such as Czechoslovakia) were not in any agreement.

10. Paragraph 11—There is no evidence that the possession of the atomic bomb was what caused President Truman to take the positions he did. Further, the comment that the Russians could "go to hell" is taken out of context. There could be any number of reasons why Truman said this. Relevant Information #1 shows a fuller context for the comment.

11. Paragraph 12—This is a *post hoc* fallacy (p. 6, "Guide to Critical Thinking"). The fact (which is also questionable) that the Soviets tightened their grip on eastern Europe after 1947 does not mean that they tightened it because of stronger American policy. Maybe the Soviets tightened up due to the failure of their own policy of flexibility in eastern Europe. The evidence of flexibility in eastern Europe, moreover, is sketchy and is challenged by contrary evidence by Interpretation B.

INTERPRETATION B

12. Paragraph 1—"Amazingly" indicates *ad hominem* arguing (p. 14, "Guide to Critical Thinking").

13. Paragraph 2—The weakness of Germany after World War II does not preclude Russian fear of her in the future. Interpretation B does nothing to prove that the Russians were not concerned about eastern Europe as a buffer to future German attacks.

14. Paragraph 3—Did Churchill (endnote 1) tell Stalin that "controlling interest" only applied to wartime?

15. Paragraph 4—The argument that the Russians "would have taken eastern Europe no matter what" could be looked at as a false scenario. The evidence presented, however, does support the charge.

16. Paragraph 5—The Soviet signature on the Declaration could be the most important issue, but that is a matter of opinion. Interpretation A has argued that Stalin may have viewed the Declaration as a public relations maneuver to please the eastern European voters in America.

17. Paragraph 7—These points show a side of the Polish question which Interpretation A failed to bring out—the fallacy of special pleading (p. 11, "Guide to Critical Thinking") by Interpretation A. On the other hand, Interpretation B likewise does not deal with the arguments and evidence that the Poles were responsible for the problems.

INTERPRETATION B

18. Paragraph 9—Interpretation B argues that there are significant differences between the spheres of influence of America and England and the sphere of influence of Russia in eastern Europe. A lot of the weight of this argument rests on the evidence in endnote 11, however. This only presents a study by Americans of political conditions in eastern Europe under the Soviets. We need more direct evidence than this.

19. Paragraph 10—The appeasement argument is a comparison. Are the two cases similar enough to justify this conclusion?

Lesson 22: Was the United States Right to Get Involved in the Vietnam War?

Objectives

To find the main idea
To recognize value claims and unstated assumptions
To evaluate evidence
To evaluate cause and effect
To evaluate comparisons
To evaluate generalizations
To evaluate debate reasoning
To evaluate proof by evidence
To relate relevant information to hypotheses

Teaching Ideas

The "Opinion Survey on War" is an optional exercise to begin the lesson. It will clarify value positions but will take some time to go through. Consider discussing only a few of the statements.

Have the students read the introduction and question them on it. This topic tends to be confusing to some students. Have them read the two viewpoints and fill in the question sheet. Then have them discuss their answers in small groups and, finally, as a class.

EXTENDING THE LESSON

An alternative procedure is to divide the class into seven groups and assign each group one of the questions below. The group has ten minutes to make an evaluation of each interpretation's argument on the question and write an answer to the question. Have each group report its conclusions to the class.

QUESTIONS

1. Was the United States right to help the French?

2. Were Diem and the United States justified in preventing the 1956 elections from being held?

3. What kind of leader was Ho Chi Minh?

4. Did the war against Diem's government originate in South Vietnam or North Vietnam?

5. Did military firepower (including bombing) bring the United States close to victory or cause American defeat?

6. What were the main reasons that American citizens opposed the war?

7. Should the United States have pushed harder for negotiations and a compromise settlement early in the war (in the 1950s and 1960s)?

Suggested Answers

INTERPRETATION A

Follow up with an essay assignment on the Vietnam War, either with or without further research required.

These are suggested answers to the question sheet.

1. There are many possible ways to state the main point of Interpretation A. One suggestion is: The United States was wrong to get involved in the Vietnam War, a war which destroyed much of Vietnamese society.

2. Comparison reasoning

   Many reasonable answers could be given. The author is making the point that Washington was popular because he was the leader of an independence movement. Since Ho was also the leader of an independence movement, he must also have been popular. Are there significant differences between the two cases?

3. The evidence in endnote 5

   P—Primary, it is from that time period

   R—No apparent reason to distort

   O—No other evidence is supporting

   P—Private

   The CIA's lack of reason to distort lends credibility to this evidence. It seems that the Vietminh probably would have won the scheduled election. One thing we would like to know is the context of the evidence.

4. 1956 Election—One possible answer

   Premise—The Vietminh were promised a nationwide election in the Geneva Agreement, but Diem and the United States prevented the election from taking place.

   Premise—Those who break agreements are wrong.

   Conclusion—The United States and Diem were wrong in the Vietnam War.

5. There are several possible weaknesses in this line of reasoning.

   —Diem and the United States did not sign the agreement on elections.

   —There may be some cases when breaking an agreement is not wrong.

6. Cause-and-effect reasoning

   The students must identify the cause (Diem's policies) and the effect (war between the Vietcong and Diem). Then they have to assess how well the author shows the connection between the cause and the effect. Interpretation A argues that many South Vietnamese hated Diem's policies and implies that rebellion grew out of this hatred. One question we could ask is: How do we know that some other factor (like infiltration from North Vietnam) was not more important as a cause of the guerrilla war?

7. Sample reasoning

   "Large numbers of innocent civilians were killed by American soldiers."

   Evaluation: The evidence used to support this refers to number of civilians killed compared to number of Vietcong killed. "Large numbers" of civilians would have been killed if large numbers of Vietcong were also killed (which is probably true).

8. Possible weakness

   One *New York Times* article does not provide proof that the Administration "continually lied to the American people."

INTERPRETATION B

9. Main point of Interpretation B: (one possible answer)

   The tragedy of the Vietnam War is not that the United States fought, but that it did not fight to win.

10. Reasoning

    Debating

11. Evidence in paragraph 4, endnote 1

    It is a secondary source. From where did this author get this idea? We have to see some evidence from the participants at Geneva before we accept this argument.

12. The key to paragraph 6 is the evidence for North Vietnamese control of the war given in endnote 4. If the evidence is weak, the argument is weak; if strong, the argument is strong. The evidence is primary and there are three statements which corroborate each other. Defectors may, however, have a reason to distort about their former group.

INTERPRETATION B

13. Assumption

Military leaders are better at plotting strategy in war than are civilian leaders.

14. Proof by evidence

The students must decide whether the evidence proves the argument made by Interpretation B. This evidence lends support to the argument that the Vietcong were decimated in the Tet Offensive, but it does not prove it. Maybe the Vietcong deliberately reduced the number of their attacks to prepare for another offensive.

15. The evidence for the executions at Hue is strong. Even though there is no corroborating evidence, the captured Vietcong document is primary, private, and its authors have no reason to distort.

16. Argument in paragraph 14

This is an interesting argument. When a side in a war decides to attack through conventional invasion, does that mean that side was losing its guerrilla war?

RELEVANT INFORMATION

17. Relevant Information—Possible answers

#1 favors Interpretation B; #2 favors Interpretation A; #3 favors Interpretation B; #4 gives support to both viewpoints; #5 favors Interpretation A

Lesson 23: Evaluating Evidence on McCarthyism and the Red Scare

Objectives

To evaluate evidence

Teaching Ideas

This is a reinforcement lesson on evaluating evidence (see lessons 2, 10, and 17). Students should fill in strengths and weaknesses, discuss answers in small groups, if appropriate, and then discuss as a class.

Suggested Answers

1. McCarthy speech

STRENGTHS

- McCarthy has supporting evidence (O) for his claim that there were Communists in government.

WEAKNESSES

- McCarthy is not a primary source (P); he has a reason to lie (R) to help his political career; and it is a public statement. Actually McCarthy did not have a list at all. He had a letter with some numbers in it.

2. Roy Cohn

STRENGTHS

- Cohn is a primary source (P).

WEAKNESSES

- Cohn has a reason to lie (R) to defend his boss; there is no other (O) evidence; and it is a public statement.

3. Lunch discussion

STRENGTHS

- The three men are primary sources (P); they verify each others' (O) stories; and it is difficult to believe they made the story up (R) since they were friends of McCarthy and since the story does not seem to help them in any way.

WEAKNESSES

- It is a public statement (P).

4. Book

STRENGTHS

- Leuchtenburg has no reason to lie (R) as far as we can tell, except that most writers and historians do not like McCarthy, so Leuchtenburg might be prejudiced.

WEAKNESSES

- It is not a primary source (P); there is no other (O) evidence supporting this claim; and it is a public statement.

5. Earl Browder

STRENGTHS
- Browder is a primary source (P) regarding who he did or did not talk to.

WEAKNESSES
- Browder gives no other (O) evidence to support his claim; it is a public statement; and either Browder or Lattimore is lying (R), unless Browder forgot about the meeting. It is hard to believe that Lattimore made up the story about meeting Browder. On the other hand, Browder has great incentive to lie. If Lattimore was in the Communist Party, Browder would want to show that he was not. Students should remember that Browder, as a Communist, may have qualms about sticking to the rules of telling the truth under oath, when those rules were made by a system he is pledged to overthrow. It is very likely that Browder is lying.

6. Letter

STRENGTHS
- It is a primary source (P); there is no reason to lie (R); and it is private (P).

WEAKNESSES
- There is no other (O) evidence supporting the letter.

SUMMARY
- This is very strong evidence, since Lattimore incriminates himself in it. He did not know anyone else would read it. Lattimore was convicted of perjury (lying under oath) for his previous statement after this letter was presented.

7. Whittaker Chambers

STRENGTHS
- Chambers might be a primary source (P), but it is unclear whether he knew Hiss personally.

WEAKNESSES
- Chambers has a reason to lie (R) to gain public acclaim by turning in a Communist during a time of fear of Communism; he presents no other (O) evidence to support his claim; and it is a public statement.

Lesson 24: Analyzing Cause and Effect on Urban Riots

Objectives

To evaluate cause and effect

Teaching Ideas

Begin the lesson by having students fill in the table, predicting where riots will occur. Have students discuss their answers in small groups. Bring the class back together and ask for a show of hands to see how many students feel there would be a riot in each of the four situations. Then read the actual results of each situation in the Suggested Answers. The point is that you cannot always predict dramatic events based on the information you have.

Tell the students to look back at the situations on the handout and the reasons for their choices. Have them work in small groups to make lists of the factors which contributed to riots in the 1960s. Bring the class back together, ask the groups to read their lists, and write the factors on the blackboard. (Many factors could be listed, but emphasize the following: police-crowd antagonism; high unemployment; frustration; white owners of businesses in black ghettoes; good weather, generally in the summer; political group involvement.)

Now you can switch to either the section on cause and effect or the National Commission report. The list of possible causes generated from the table will be helpful in evaluating the National Commission's argument.

For the section on cause and effect, have the students fill in which argument is strongest (question 5), have them discuss their answers in small groups, and then discuss as a class. Use the same procedure for the questions on the Commission's report.

Suggested Answers

SITUATIONS

The answers are the actual results; riots occurred in situations 1, 3, and 4. Some rioting occurred in situation 2, but it was not a full-scale riot.

SITUATION 1

- A fifteen-year-old black youth attacked the policeman with a knife. The officer shot and killed the boy. The next day the Progressive Labor Movement, a Marxist-Leninist organization, passed out leaflets charging the police with brutality. The following day the Congress on Racial Equality, a civil rights organization, marched on the police station where the crowd clashed with police. Full-scale rioting followed.

SITUATION 2

- A crowd gathered in front of the store, broke the store windows, and threw rocks at passing cars. The next day the store was set on fire by a Molotov cocktail. Several persons were injured, but order was restored.

SITUATION 3

- A crowd of black spectators gathered and more police officers arrived at the scene. Full scale rioting resulted for two nights.

SITUATION 4

- A crowd gathered and more police were called to the scene. A young black woman, who was accused of spitting on the police, was dragged by police into the street. After the police left, the crowd started throwing rocks at cars, beating up motorists, and setting cars on fire. Community leaders were not able to restore calm. The next day large crowds, opposed by only a few police, destroyed white property in Watts, a business district two miles from the location of the original incident. The National Guard was called in. The result of the riot was 34 people killed, hundreds wounded, and $35 million in damage.

CONNECTION

5. Connecting cause and effect

   Based on the criterion of connecting poverty (the proposed cause) to the riots (the effect), the best argument is B. This argument connects poverty to frustration and desire for consumer goods, which provide a motive for rioting. In addition, it connects poverty to unemployment, which leads to a bored, frustrated crowd, which connects to rioting.

   Historian A explains how poverty leads to hopelessness, which could, in fact, be the main cause of the riots. We would like to see more explanation of how hopelessness would lead to rioting. The information on Watts and Detroit is irrelevant to proving poverty as the main cause.

   Historian C describes poverty in more detail than the other two but does not explain how the resulting frustration led to the riots.

NATIONAL COMMISSION REPORT

6. The Commission felt that American society in general was responsible for the poverty of the ghetto, and the poverty and conditions led to the riots. Students should question the connection between poverty and the riots. The connection is reasonable but students might argue that it should be explained more fully (which it was in the 250,000 word report).

From the list of possible causes generated in the first section, students should mention other possible causes for riots.

7. Riots can be stopped by ending racial discrimination and segregation. The commission also implied that the problems or riots would not be ended until the problems of poverty, hopelessness, and unemployment in the ghettos were solved.

Student opinions of these recommendations will vary.

Lesson 25: Identifying and Evaluating Types of Reasoning

Objectives

To identify and evaluate cause and effect
To identify and evaluate generalizations
To identify and evaluate comparisons
To identify and evaluate proof by evidence
To identify and evaluate proof by eliminating
   alternatives

Teaching Ideas

Have students fill in the answers individually and share their answers in small groups where they can help one another. Discuss their answers as a class. Since there are several types of reasoning possible for some items, listen for the reasons behind student answers.

Suggested Answers

1. Superintendent letter

   TYPE
   • Comparison

   EVALUATION
   • There are very significant differences between following union leaders in a strike and following political leaders in genocide. This is a very poor analogy.

2. Borrowed the bike

   TYPE
   • Proof by eliminating alternatives

   EVALUATION
   • We need to be sure that Christine and Leanne really are the only ones who can ride the bike, and that Leanne really could not have borrowed it all day.

3. President Eisenhower

   TYPE
   • Cause and effect; generalization

   EVALUATION
   • There is a reasonable connection between public opinion and changing his views, but it needs to be explained more fully. Also, there are other possible causes (such as the Democrats controlled Congress, so he was forced to compromise).

4. McCarthy's charges

   TYPE
   • Proof by evidence; generalization

   EVALUATION
   • The argument assumes that the firing of people McCarthy accused is evidence that they were security risks and McCarthy was right to accuse them. Actually, it might be that McCarthy's charges themselves caused the people to be fired (cause and effect).

5. Welfare length

Type   • Generalization

Evaluation   • *Time* probably got the information from the government department which runs welfare. We do not know how large or representative the sample is.

6. Governor Faubus

Type   • Cause and effect

Evaluation   • Both of the causes mentioned make sense in connecting the opposition to integration. Also, the argument considers several causes. There are, however, other possible causes; for example, maybe he really believed integration was a bad policy at that time.

7. Stock crash of 1987

Type   • Comparison; cause and effect

Evaluation   • There are some important differences between 1929 and 1987. For example, the Securities and Exchange Commission is supposed to prevent stock fraud and abuses such as buying on margin; the FDIC insures bank deposits; and the government pays benefits to unemployed people.

8. Environmental statement

Type   • Comparison

Evaluation   • Corporate pollution seems as bad as or worse than human pollution. One minor difference might be that we prevent individuals from relieving themselves in public areas for reasons of privacy.

9. 1968 election

Type   • Generalization; proof by evidence

Evaluation   • It is a complete sample so it is a very strong generalization.

10. Welfare benefits

Type   • Comparison

Evaluation   • The cost of living was much higher in Alaska than it was in Alabama in 1987. Students may not know about cost of living, but they should at least ask about such differences.

Lesson 26: Types of Reasoning about Civil Rights

Objectives

To identify and evaluate cause and effect
To identify generalizations
To identify and evaluate comparisons
To identify proof by evidence
To identify proof by authority
To identify irrelevant-proof fallacy

Teaching Ideas

This is intended to be a short reinforcement lesson on types of reasoning. Have students fill in the answers individually, share their answers in small groups and discuss as a class. You can shorten the lesson by skipping the small group step.

Suggested Answers
"Brown v. Board of Education"

1. Separate schools violate the equal protection clause (they are unconstitutional).

2. C

3. B

4. C

5. B

Southern Manifesto

6. D

7. C   How many is case after case? How many cases did they sample?

8. B

9. Some historians argue that the Manifesto encouraged resistance to integration, including violent resistance. When students give their answers, ask other students to evaluate their causal reasoning. They will have to remember the evaluation questions: Is there a good connection? Are there other possible causes?

Montgomery Bus Boycott

10. C

11. B

12. There seems to be a logical connection between the boycott and the bus company almost going bankrupt, since the company would lose a lot of money without most of its riders. There might be other causes for bankruptcy, such as poor management, but the boycott was likely the main cause.

King and Gandhi

13. A

14. The arguer shows one way that the two men were similar, and this similarity is important. There are differences in culture, geography, leadership, and personality to take into consideration if the person extended the argument to say that nonviolent resistance was the main reason for King's success (as with Gandhi).

PROFESSOR CLEMENS

15. E

Lesson 27: Why Did Blacks Have Less Upward Mobility Than Immigrants in Boston from 1880 to 1970?

Objectives

To evaluate cause and effect
To relate relevant information to hypotheses

Teaching Ideas

Have students read the overview and ask them questions about social class, mobility, white collar and blue collar jobs. Ask them why they think blacks had lower mobility than immigrants, and write their hypotheses on the chalkboard.

After students read the historians, go over the tables with them, explaining areas that might be difficult. For example, Table 1 deals with housing segregation. If all the Italians lived in one neighborhood, they would be highly segregated, getting a score of 100. If they were spread evenly throughout the city, then they would get a very low number, say 11.

As students work through the tables, you will have to circulate around the room to help students who have questions.

After students have filled in the evaluation chart for the historians, have them discuss their answers in groups of three, then discuss them as a class.

You can make the lesson less difficult by cueing students to look at specific tables or information for each of the interpretations. For example, tell students to look at Table 4 for Theory A. See the Suggested Answers for suggestions of which tables or information go with which viewpoints.

Suggested Answers

THEORY A

Theory A's argument is weakened by Table 4, which shows that Northern blacks did no better than those from the South.

THEORY B

Theory B's argument is strengthened by Table 10 and information 12. None of the information weakens this view.

THEORY C

Theory C's argument is weakened by Table 2, which shows that blacks went to school as much as whites, and blacks went to school more than some immigrant groups but got worse jobs.

THEORY D	Theory D's view is weakened by Tables 1 and 5. These tables show that a highly geographically segregated group (Jewish immigrants) did well occupationally, while a largely geographically non-segregated group (Irish immigrants) did poorly. Thus, geographic segregation could not be a deciding factor in job mobility.
THEORY E	Theory E's view is weakened by Tables 2, 9, and 11. Tables 9 and 11 cast doubt upon, but do not disprove, the assumption that blacks had larger families. If blacks had fewer children in 1960, and if the infant mortality for blacks was higher in 1900, then it is questionable whether blacks had larger families. Table 2 shows that blacks went to school as much as whites but got worse jobs.
THEORY F	Theory F's view is weakened by Tables 2, 3, and 6 and information 13 and 14. Tables 3 and 6 show that in 1880 blacks had more stable families than the Irish but got worse jobs. Information 13 and 14 show that in 1960 blacks had the same percentage of broken families as whites, but got worse jobs. Table 2 makes us question the argument that family instability leads to lower educational achievement. Why did blacks stay in school longer if they did not do as well?
THEORY G	Theory G's view is weakened by Tables 4 and 10 and by information 12. Table 4 shows that blacks came from many backgrounds. Even blacks from overseas did poorly in the job market compared to non-blacks. Foreign blacks who did not experience slavery had different cultures from American blacks. The increase in semi-skilled jobs for blacks in 1940 suggests that when labor was needed (as in World War II) then black culture did not stand in the way of blacks getting jobs.
SUMMARY	Overall, Theory B's interpretation is strongest, based on the information presented in this lesson.

Lesson 28: What Are the Causes and Effects of More Women Working Outside the Home?

Objectives

To identify and evaluate cause and effect
To identify the correlation-as-cause fallacy
To relate relevant information to hypotheses

Teaching Ideas

Have the students answer the first two questions about possible causes and effects of more women working outside the home and write their answers on the chalkboard. Their answers will help students see causes other than the ones proposed in the lesson.

Continue by having students proceed through Part II of the lesson, answering the questions by referring to the tables. The general question of discrimination against females should generate some differences of opinion in the class.

After Part II is discussed, have students revise their hypotheses by examining the tables (and graph) in Part III. Question students about their causal reasoning.

Suggested Answers

Part II

HISTORIAN A

1. Table 1
2. Table 3
3. Cause and effect—The argument is that women working causes divorce.
4. Correlation as cause—A (women working) and B (divorce) went up at the same time, so A caused B. It is just as likely that B (divorce) caused A (more women had to work to support themselves).
5. Information that women's participation in the labor force significantly increased before the divorce rate increased or evidence showing that particular divorces were due to wives working would strengthen Historian A. Can this type of evidence be found?

HISTORIAN B

6. Table 3 (births per 1,000 population is decreasing)
7. Cause and effect—Smaller families have caused (one cause) more women to work.
8. This argument has the same weakness that Historian A's argument has. It commits the correlation-as-cause fallacy (p. 6, "Guide to Critical Thinking").

We need more information that would show the connection between the supposed cause and the effect. Without more information we could as easily conclude that more women working outside the home led to smaller families. A comparison of tables 1 and 3 also shows that the correlation is not uniform. In 1950 and 1960 the number of births was *higher* while women were working. This suggests that other factors are involved.

HISTORIAN C

9. Table 2

10. Table 2 supports the argument. The table shows that women's earnings have actually fallen as a percentage of men's earnings.

HISTORIAN D

11. Table 4 tends to weaken the argument since it shows that a major reason women earn less than men is that they work fewer years. There are fewer women working in the seniority positions. In occupations where pay rises mainly with seniority (years of experience), women will get a lower salary. The problem is compounded because when women leave the workforce to raise children they often return to different positions where their previous years of service do not count.

On the other hand, Table 4 (in conjunction with Table 2) could be seen to support the argument in that as women have worked a higher percentage of years compared to men, their pay has dropped compared to men! This could show discrimination.

12. Women more often quit their jobs to raise children.

13. As explained above, women might receive lower pay due to the hiatus in many women's working career to raise children. It could, however, be due to a number of other factors. After divorce, many women are forced to work while they also have custody of the children. This forces them into working only certain hours which translates into lower paying occupations and part-time employment.

Part III
WHY MORE WOMEN WORK

A. Possible causes from the tables

—Smaller families (Table 5)

—Antidiscrimination laws and affirmative action—possibly shown in the higher percentage of women in the professional category (Table 6)

—Change in attitude about mothers working (Table 7)

—More married women working as second incomes to their working husband (Table 8)

EFFECTS OF WOMEN
WORKING

B. The list could be much longer—students should generate a lot of effects.

—Women have less leisure time (since they seem to be doing the same amount of household work on top of their paid employment—Graph 9)

—Women may have more self-esteem from working

—Children have less supervision

—Men may take traditional female roles

—Women may have more stress (possibly smoke more)

—Less economic domination by men

WHY WOMEN RECEIVE
LOWER PAY

C. Possible causes

—Despite some advances by women into traditionally male occupations, such as management and highly paid professions, most are funneled into traditional female service jobs (Table 10). The implication is that discrimination causes it. Notice how this information supports Historian D's claim by offering a different perspective than Table 4.

—Table 6 also shows that, despite gains in the area of management, women increased dramatically in clerical, sales, and manual jobs.

—It may be that women working for second incomes will accept lower pay because their pay is additional, not central to the family's survival. Women in this situation are also more likely to work part time, which translates into lower hourly rates and few, if any, benefits.

—Divorced women may be forced suddenly into the role of breadwinner without time to plan a career. These women may be forced into lower paying, less desirable jobs. This effect of divorce is an important factor in the "feminization of poverty"—an increasingly higher percentage of the poor are women and children.

Lesson 29: Was the Kennedy Assassination a Conspiracy?

Objectives

To evaluate evidence
To evaluate cause and effect

Teaching Ideas

One way to use this lesson is to have students read both viewpoints and write down which viewpoint they agree with and why. Then either have students debate which view is stronger or discuss the two viewpoints as a class. In either case, the strengths and weaknesses of evidence should emerge.

A second method is to have students read only Interpretation A and have students write down whether they are convinced by it. Most students should be convinced. Ask them why and then ask them to anticipate arguments that Interpretation B might make.

A good way to follow up is to have students research the event further and draw new conclusions based on their research.

Selected Analyses

Interpretation A

The evidence in paragraphs 2, 3, and 4 is all circumstantial—it does not really show there was a conspiracy. The best evidence is from Rose Sharime. But we would prefer more than one source on the Ruby-Oswald connection.

The evidence in paragraph 5 that the shots were too close together in time is impressive, but Interpretation B will explain that one "magic bullet" caused several wounds simultaneously.

One point that Interpretation B does not refute is the pristine condition of the magic bullet (paragraph 7).

It seems logical that the head should have gone forward and the test confirms it.

The large number of eyewitnesses (paragraph 9) who say they heard shots and saw smoke coming from the grassy knoll are important and not refuted by Interpretation B.

The argument in paragraph 10 is highly speculative. There "could" have been surgery done; there is no hard evidence that surgery was done. The surgery would have had to fool the doctors at Bethesda into believing that it was a bullet wound.

Interpretation B

The evidence in paragraph 2 that Jack Ruby was at the police station at the right time by chance certainly weakens the argument of Ruby killing Oswald as a Mafia hit. But who knows exactly what happened? Maybe Ruby was there earlier and decided to leave and come back. Maybe he planned to kill Oswald later but saw a good opportunity and took it.

The evidence in paragraph 3 is very important. If there was another assassin, where are the bullet fragments from the other's weapon?

The evidence in paragraph 5 shows that the magic bullet could have inflicted all those wounds, but it does not prove that it did. Interpretation B does not account for the pristine nature of the bullet, it just argues that it is less likely to be damaged if slowed down (paragraph 6).

The evidence in paragraph 8 is also very important, showing the entrance wounds from the rear. How can the grassy knoll adherents respond to this evidence?

Paragraph 10 provides a test with the very opposite results from the test explained in Interpretation A. Unless we know more about the tests, or have them redone, we cannot make a decision about the results.

Interpretation B (paragraph 11) weakens a couple of points on the grassy knoll but ignores the numerous eyewitness accounts supporting shots and smoke coming from there. It is important to point out this omission to your students.

The evidence provided by Interpretation B in paragraphs 3 (bullet fragments only from Oswald's rifle) and 8 (entrance wounds from the rear) are very strong. You might want to assign students to find out how supporters of the conspiracy view, such as David Lifton, deal with these points.

Part I—Individual Skills

Q Label each item below with the appropriate letter.

S A **source** of information is given.

N **No** source of information is given.

_____1. Richard Nixon defeated George McGovern in the 1972 Presidential Election.

_____2. The United States and the Soviet Union both rely on the strategy of deterrence to prevent a nuclear attack.

_____3. Lyndon Johnson defeated Barry Goldwater in the 1964 Election because Goldwater appeared to many voters to be too radical, according to William E. Leuchtenburg in *The Unfinished Century: America Since 1900*.

_____4. Four students were killed and eleven wounded when Ohio National Guardsmen opened fire on them on May 4, 1970, at Kent State University.

Q Evaluate the strengths and weaknesses of the following pieces of evidence. Remember the four criteria for evaluating evidence.

—President Nixon told the newspapers he did not try to protect himself by covering up the Watergate Scandal.

5. Strengths:

6. Weaknesses:

—John Dean testified to a congressional investigating committee that President Nixon was involved in covering up the Watergate Scandal. Dean said that Nixon paid money to the burglars to keep them quiet. Dean was Nixon's legal counsel (Nixon's lawyer).

7. Strengths:

8. Weaknesses:

[Continued on next page.]

[Continued from previous page.]

—The tape recordings of conversations which President Nixon made for his own use in writing his memoirs (the other people in the White House did not know that their conversations with the President were being taped) contain statements by Nixon that money should be paid to the men caught in the Watergate burglary so that the men would not tell that the Nixon Reelection Committee was involved in the scandal.

9. Strengths:

10. Weaknesses:

—Historian Winthrop Jordan said in his book *The United States* that by 1980 most Americans viewed Jimmy Carter as a weak, indecisive, and ineffective president.

11. Strengths:

12. Weaknesses:

—Seven people testified under oath that they saw Sacco at the scene of the murder for which Sacco and Vanzetti were being tried.

13. Strengths:

14. Weaknesses:

 Evaluate the following cause-and-effect arguments.

15. The 1964 tax cut was a brilliant success. In the next year and a half consumer

[Continued on next page.]

[Continued from previous page.]

spending, with the extra money left over from taxes, rose dramatically. Consequently, the gross national product soared and the government actually took in more money (a lower tax rate but on higher incomes).

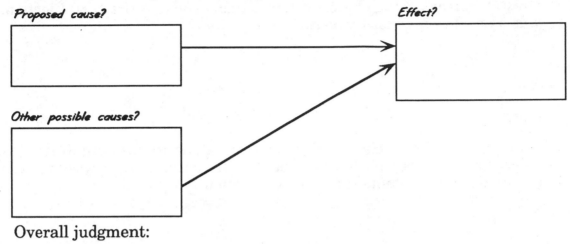

Overall judgment:

16. The controversial and violent 1968 Democratic Convention in Chicago divided the Democratic Party and paved the way for the Republican victory.

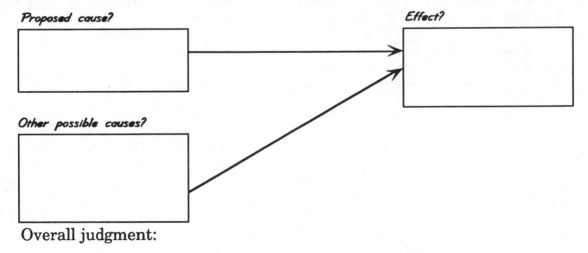

Overall judgment:

[Continued on next page.]

[Continued from previous page.]

 Evaluate the following generalizations:

17. Only 52 percent of the eligible voters actually voted in the 1980 Election. This was a new low in voter turnout.

18. John says that Lee Harvey Oswald acted alone in assassinating President Kennedy. Bill responds, "Most people know the assassination was a conspiracy." (Evaluate Bill's statement as a generalization.)

 Evaluate the following comparisons:

19. Americans were much better off economically in 1960 than they had been at the end of World War II. The Gross National Product more than doubled from $213.6 billion in 1945 to $503.7 billion in 1960.

20. Getting involved in El Salvador would be a big mistake. It will turn into another Vietnam.

 Identify the unstated assumption in each of the following.

"The New Deal programs were radical. After all, look at all the programs to help the unemployed and poor at the expense of the taxpayers."

[Continued on next page.]

[Continued from previous page.]

_____21.   What is the assumption in this argument?

A.   All government programs are radical.

B.   The New Deal was a failure.

C.   Government programs to help the poor at the expense of the taxpayers are radical.

D.   The government should not have programs.

"Getting off the Gold Standard in the 1930s was a big mistake which hurt our economy. After all, staying on the Gold Standard helps keep the supply of money stable, which, in the long run, prevents inflation."

_____22.   What is the assumption?

A.   The Gold Standard made us prosperous in the 1920s.

B.   A stable supply of money is an important factor in having a good economy.

C.   When the economy is weak, the supply of money is not stable.

D.   Staying on the Gold Standard helps international trade.

 Identify the type of reasoning (write the correct letter) and evaluate it in each of the following arguments.

Types of Reasoning

A.   Cause and Effect   C.   Comparison

B.   Generalization   D.   Proof by Authority

Reporter—(To one of the crew of the *Columbia* shuttle before its second trip.) "Isn't being in the shuttle for the second trip more dangerous? After all, it's a used spaceship now."

Astronaut—"No, it isn't more dangerous. It's like a new car that has been driven around the block. Now the bugs have been worked out of it."

_____23.   Type of Reasoning by the Astronaut

24.   Evaluation:

[Continued on next page.]

[Continued from previous page.]

"By 1936 the New Deal helped the country to begin to recover from the Great Depression. National income had risen from $47 billion in 1932 to $70 billion in 1936, while industrial production had doubled in the same time period. Unemployment fell from 12 million in 1932 to 9 million in 1936."

_____25. Type of Reasoning

26. Evaluation:

"The reason the United States got into World War I was because German submarines sank our ships."

_____27. Type of Reasoning

28. Evaluation:

(A statement by a person on the issue of tuition tax credits, [public assistance] to families who send their children to private schools.) "If you want to join a private country club, as opposed to a public one, that is your privilege. But, you don't expect your neighbor to foot the bill. Why should those who decide to send their children to private schools rather than public ones receive assistance from their neighbors?"

_____29. Type of Reasoning

30. Evaluation:

"In 1932 we elected the Democrat Roosevelt and during his administration we got into World War II. Then we had the Democrat Truman and the Korean War. In the 1960s we had the Democrats Kennedy and Johnson and wound up in the Vietnam War. Can we afford another Democrat?"

_____31. Type of Reasoning

[Continued on next page.]

[Continued from previous page.]

32.   Evaluation:

"The United States could have stayed out of World War I much longer if we had an embargo on goods shipped to England and Germany. After all, when we did that under similar circumstances in the early 1800s we stayed out of the War of 1812 for five years longer."

_____33.   Type of Reasoning

34.   Evaluation:

"The main reason for the Great Depression was the uneven distribution of wealth in the 1920s. Most people prospered in the 1920s, but rich people prospered more. In 1929 rich people had a higher percentage of the total wealth of the country than they had in 1920. Since the poorer classes did not have as much money as they could otherwise have had, these poorer people couldn't buy the surplus goods that were produced. The country was left with overproduction which plunged it into the depression."

_____35.   Type of Reasoning

36.   Evaluation:

Q Identify the type of reasoning in each of the following by writing the letter of the appropriate answer on the line.

A.	Cause and Effect	C.	Comparison
B.	Generalization	D.	Proof by Authority

_____37.   John F. Kennedy, being a Catholic, was the Al Smith of the 1960s.

_____38.   The race riots of the 1960s were instigated by outside agitators who got blacks angry at whites.

[Continued on next page.]

[Continued from previous page.]

_____39.   "I checked on your theory that the New Deal was a communist conspiracy. Frank Friedel, a noted expert on the New Deal says that there were few communists in the New Deal, and that few programs were designed to communize the economy."

_____40.   Crowds at sporting events were larger in the 1920s than previously.

_____41.   John F. Kennedy was influenced to take a strong stand to reduce poverty by his experiences in the West Virginia primary campaign and by reading *The Other America* by Michael Harrington.

Part II Mixed Problems

 Read the following interpretation of the United States entry into World War I and answer questions 42–48 based on the interpretation.

Historian Z (1934)

(1) The reasons for the United States decision to go to war in April 1917 were many. The most important of these, however, was the attitude of mind in this country—the product of British propaganda. People under the influence of the propaganda came to look upon the struggle of 1914–1918 as a simple conflict between the forces of good and evil. In the minds of American leaders there developed a blind hatred of everything German. After this hatred had destroyed American neutrality, it created a willingness to sacrifice American youth in a war that attempted to punish the hated nation.

(2) The propaganda influenced President Wilson to such an extent that he overcame the American desire for peace with his own desire for a British-French victory. It caused him to be unneutral until it was too late for him to exert pressure to bring about a just peace.

(3) In order to remove the causes for German submarine warfare, some Americans wanted pressure exerted on Great Britain to force her to relax the illegal blockade of the Central Powers

(Germany's side). Wilson, however, refused to do anything which would embarrass the Allies (Britain and France, mainly). Many Americans wanted an embargo on munitions; Wilson objected. Secretary of State Bryan prohibited (prevented) loans to the warring nations; Wilson personally defeated the measure. The President's partisanship was so apparent that even the British stated: "During the period while America was neutral all the issues in dispute between England and America were decided as England wished."

(4) The public was told that the argument with Great Britain about freedom of the seas was concerned with property while that with Germany was concerned with lives. This served to hide the actual claims on the part of Mr. Wilson which today seem almost fantastic. The issue was not the right of Americans to travel on American ships in peaceful waters. And no Americans were killed on American ships prior to February 1917 under circumstances which would have justified war. What he was insist-

[Continued on next page.]

Historian Z

[Continued from previous page.]

ing on, at the price of war, was the right of Americans to travel in the war zone (1) on foreign ships of belligerent nationality (British ships), (2) on foreign ships which were armed, and (3) on foreign ships carrying munitions and other supplies of war. Wilson never compromised on these rights. Once Wilson got us into the war he justified it not as a defense of freedom of the seas, but as a great crusade to end all wars.

(5) In the last analysis the American government was forced to join the Allies in 1917 because it had already surrendered to them its material, diplomatic, and moral support. Norway, Sweden, Denmark, and Holland refrained from such unneutral conduct and, in spite of the fact that they suffered a great deal more than did this country, they escaped becoming involved.

(6) Certainly if the United States had imitated the self-restraint of these other countries, she also could have remained in peace. The reason she did not act in the same way was because of the tremendously effective British propaganda campaign. In Europe the agents of British propaganda had to compete with the propagandists of Germany and the other Central Powers. In the United States, however, they had a free field. This climate of opinion influenced finance, industry, and government.

(7) To some, the history of the "neutrality" period demonstrates that the United States cannot keep out of war. But the facts do not bear out any such contention. What it does prove is that it is impossible to be unneutral and keep out of war.

_____42. What is the main point of this argument?

A. British propaganda was wrong.

B. President Wilson was not really neutral—he insisted on ridiculous rights for Americans.

C. British propaganda pushed America into the war.

D. The United States should have given more support to Germany and the other Central Powers.

_____43. What is an *unstated* assumption in the argument?

A. Propaganda can influence a country to take unneutral actions.

B. The British had a free field to use propaganda in the United States.

C. Norway, Sweden, Denmark, and Holland were all able to remain neutral during the war.

D. Presidents should insist on citizens' rights.

[Continued on next page.]

[Continued from previous page.]

Q What type of reasoning is used in each of the following sentences or quoted phrases from the argument?

A. Sample	C. Cause and Effect
B. Comparison	D. Proof by Example

_____44. "The mind of this country" hated Germany.

_____45. American attitudes toward Germany were the product of British propaganda.

_____46. "Many Americans wanted an embargo."

Q Consider the Evidence

_____47. In which sentence is evidence presented?

_____48. Which of the following pieces of information best supports Historian Z's argument?

A. American bankers loaned money to England to invest their money profitably.

B. Secretary of State Bryan was opposed to loaning money to England.

C. President Wilson was outraged by German acts of inhumanity in Belgium. The events in Belgium were reported by British agents and correspondents.

D. President Wilson was very upset when Americans were killed on British ships. These ships were sunk by German U–boats.

Q Identify Points of View

"By the 1930s, the United States was almost the only advanced country in the world which did not have social welfare programs to protect its citizens against unemployment or other disasters. While millions of families were destitute in the early 1930s, the government seemed indifferent to their problems. President Roosevelt was determined to do something to end this neglect. Under the New Deal, he started a long overdue unemployment insurance program and a pension plan for people over 65."

_____49. This historian is most likely:

A. Favorable to Roosevelt

B. Unfavorable to Roosevelt

C. Neutral regarding Roosevelt

D. Has no opinion regarding Roosevelt

[Continued on next page.]

[Continued from previous page.]

_____50. What is an assumption in this view?
    A. The government usually messes things up.
    B. Poor people should be helped by the government.
    C. Government help for the destitute helps economic growth.
    D. The United States government could not afford to help the poor through social welfare programs before the 1930s.

TEST QUESTION ANSWERS

Teaching Ideas

You can use the test questions as they are written or you can cut parts out (such as the multiple choice options) to make them more challenging. You could also present the argument (Historian Z on World War I) in Part II without the questions and instruct students to evaluate it.

An alternate method of evaluation is to have students write essays responding to or evaluating any of the historical interpretations (Historian A or B in the various lessons) in the book.

Suggested Answers

IDENTIFY EVIDENCE

1. N
2. N
3. S
4. N

EVALUATE EVIDENCE

NIXON

5. Strengths

   Primary source

6. Weaknesses

   Reason to lie; no other evidence; public statement

DEAN

7. Strengths

   Primary source; he might gain by making this story up (lying) but it is hard to see how

8. Weaknesses

   No other evidence; public statement

NIXON TAPES

9. Strengths

   Primary source; no reason to lie; private recordings

10. Weaknesses

    No other evidence

WINTHROP JORDAN

11. Strengths

    No reason to lie

12. Weaknesses

    Not a primary source; no other evidence; it is public

SACCO

13. Strengths

    Primary source; other evidence; testified under oath (more serious if lying)

	14.	**Weaknesses**
		They might have a reason to lie (prejudice, etc.); it is public.
EVALUATE CAUSE AND EFFECT	15.	**1964 Tax Cut**
		The tax cut is well connected to larger GNP and higher incomes, however, there are other economic factors such as lower interest rates or increased exports that could have led to a larger GNP.
	16.	**1968 Democratic Convention**
		There is not much explanation of how the Convention divided the party or how a divided party would lead to the opponents winning. (Although it seems reasonable that if one party is divided the other party will more likely win.) There are a number of other factors, such as the candidates' strengths and weaknesses and the inflation rate, which also affect the outcome.
EVALUATE GENERALIZATIONS	17.	**1980 Election Vote**
		This is undoubtedly from voting results so it is a complete (thus completely representative) sample.
	18.	**Assassination of Kennedy**
		There was no sample taken, most likely. Thus, it is more like a hunch—a very poor generalization.
EVALUATE COMPARISONS	19.	**GNP Doubled**
		It looks impressive, but one difference might be the price of goods and services. If prices also doubled, Americans were not better off. Also, if the population doubled then each American was not, on average, better off. Real, per capita GNP takes in both of these differences, so it is a much better comparative measure of whether Americans were better off.
	20.	**El Salvador and Vietnam**
		The geography is different, the distance is different, the comparative size of the countries is different, among other differences. This seems like a poor comparison.
ASSUMPTIONS	21.	C
	22.	B

IDENTIFY AND EVALUATE TYPES OF REASONING REPORTER AND ASTRONAUT	23. C—Comparison
	24. The astronaut's analogy to getting the bugs out of a car seems stronger than the reporter's argument of a used spaceship. Listen for students' arguments of similarities (both pieces of technology) and differences (spaceship wears out faster) between cars and spaceships.
NEW DEAL	25. C—Comparison / A—Cause and effect
	26. Cause and effect—There is no explanation that the New Deal actually caused these improvements. That is, no connection was made, leaving this as the correlation-as-cause fallacy. There could be other causes for the improvements.
WORLD WAR I	27. A—Cause and effect
	28. Only one cause is offered (single-cause fallacy) and no explanation of how submarines caused us to enter the war.
TUITION TAX CREDITS	29. C—Comparison
	30. There are differences. For example, better education benefits society whereas country clubs are for leisure rather than society's benefit. Students may disagree on how important the differences are.
DEMOCRATS AND WARS	31. A—Cause and effect / B—Generalization
	32. Cause and effect—There is a correlation here but no explanation of a connection between the cause and the effect. It might be, contrary to this argument, that in times of crisis leading to war we tend to elect Democrats for president.
WORLD WAR I AND WAR OF 1812	33. C—Comparison
	34. The wars are similar in that both involved American shipping rights as a neutral power during a war. But there are many differences (submarines killed people; impressment, War Hawks). Also, some historians believe the embargo was a key mistake in pushing us into war.
GREAT DEPRESSION	35. A—Cause and effect / B—Generalization
	36. Cause and effect—The connection is explained well but there are other possibly more important causes that have not been eliminated.

IDENTIFY TYPES OF	37.	C
REASONING	38.	A
	39.	D
	40.	C/B
	41.	A
PART II	42.	C
ANALYZE AN ARGUMENT	43.	A
	44.	A
	45.	C
	46.	A
	47.	Last sentence of paragraph 3
	48.	C
POINT OF VIEW	49.	A
	50.	B